There's No Such Thing as a Self-Made
Man

Pralhad P. Chhabria
Founder Chairman, FINOLEX Group

VISHWAKARMA
PUBLICATIONS VP

There's No Such Thing as a Self-Made Man

First Edition: Ameya Prakashan, March 2008
Second Edition: Vishwakarma Publications, April 2014
Reprint : May 2016

Text: Saaz Aggarwal

ISBN 978-93-83572-19-9

Cover Design and Website: Focus Communications
Finolex and P. P. Chhabria family portraits: Sateesh Paknikar

Published by:
Vishwakarma Publications
283, Budhawar Peth, Near City Post,
Pune- 411 002.
Phone No: 020-20261157
Email: info@vpindia.co.in
Website: www.vpindia.co.in

Printed at : Repro India Ltd., Mumbai

₹ 250/-

Benediction

You have realized the truth, that the purpose of life is not to be happy. The purpose of life is to spread the sunshine of joy wherever you go. The purpose of life is to spread the sunbeams of love, where there is darkness of hatred and misunderstanding.

Through the witness of your life, you have shown what it is to be too great for worry, too self-controlled for anger, too strong for fear, too happy in the midst of small irritations.

You know what it is to laugh and make others laugh, to smile and make others smile.

I pray for God's choicest benedictions to be poured on you and your noble work.

Dada
(J P Vaswani)

FOREWORD

P. P. Chhabria, is an unpretentious philanthropist, an ingenious entrepreneur with exceptional business acumen, and a truly compassionate individual and visionary.

It is only a miniscule percentage of individuals, among the billions of people in the world, who have risen from nowhere to the heights that Mr. Chhabria has attained. It is hard to believe that he is barely literate, his schooling was interrupted at a very young age of 7, and that he worked as a domestic helper at the age of 12. At the age of 15, he shouldered the responsibility of his widowed mother and 9 siblings by sending them his meager savings of Rs. 30. It is from such ranks that he built Finolex, which is today the number one manufacturer of cables in India and second in PVC resin and employs more than 5000 people. What he lacked by way of formal education, he learned through hard work and life experiences and built Finolex by adhering to ethical business practices and by maintaining the highest standards in quality and service.

I had the opportunity to work with him briefly during his early years in IndusInd Enterprises & Finance Ltd. which later merged into IndusInd Bank. It was during this period that I spotted his uncanny and innate sense for numbers. His knowledge of accounting is truly remarkable. He reads balance sheets in a jiffy. He also has the supreme ability to convert difficulties and obstacles into opportunities. It is these intrinsic traits that are perhaps the secrets of his success as a businessman. His proudest moments in the industries he led, came when Finolex was presented the Harvard Business School and Economic Times Award for the Best Corporate Performance and he was recognised as one of the Hidden Champions of the World by World Link Magazine published by the World Economic Forum, Geneva.

Though untutored himself, Mr. Chhabria understands the value of education as well as anyone who has towered in studies. He has contributed munificently to Priyadarshni Academy, a prominent, internationally-recognized NGO with which I have had the pleasure of heading for nearly three decades. He was unhesitating and large-hearted in his giving.

He has created academic opportunities, which he did not himself have, especially for the under-privileged.

He first established the Finolex Academy of Management & Technology in Ratnagiri in 1996 to make education available in rural areas and to the poor to make a contribution towards an inclusive India. In the year 2000, he set up the International Institute of Information Technology in Pune for providing higher education to the young graduates of this country. He has always advocated and supported the importance of encouraging and supporting the girl child. He also started the Mukul Madhav School in the Konkan belt, a primary school to educate the children in that area.

P. P. has a remarkably down-to-earth and unassuming style, has an inner discipline for perfection. Among all these enviable human qualities, the one that stands out is his humility. It has been my privilege and honor to have known him closely for many years and to have shared countless number of hours learning from his highly laudable human attributes. He is, in many ways, a person beyond compare.

P. P. has lived a life that is worth emulating. The youth of India has much to learn from the man and his achievements. His biography should be recommended reading for all school and college going kids in India.

I wish P. P. many more years of success and achievements.

Nanik Rupani

Dedicated to the memory of my beloved
wife Mohini Chhabria

CONTENTS

1

My Interrupted Childhood

"Since I could barely read or write, I could be given only casual work. My duties included sweeping and cleaning the shop before we started the day, offering water to customers, clearing away the samples of fabric and other goods after they left, and performing any odd job I was given."

In 1947, India achieved independence from the British. In most of the large towns across India, processions of laughing, excited revellers thronged the streets. At the same time, people on both sides of this newly-created border were experiencing a wave of human turmoil, pain, and savage bloodshed never before seen in history. The British had drawn an arbitrary line through India to create the nation of Pakistan. Till today the magnitude of this episode has not been sufficiently documented or understood.

Yet in India there were many whose lives were completely untouched by this Independence. Hundreds of thousands continued with their daily tasks and routines, ignorant that an epic moment was occurring.

I, Pralhad P. Chhabria, was one of these people. I had no idea whatever that something so very important was happening around me.

1

Some mornings I would see groups of youngsters marching through the streets, waving flags and shouting slogans. Occasionally the processions took place late in the evening, and they marched holding candles. I watched them from the second-floor balcony of the house in which I lived and worked, but had no idea what the flags or slogans signified. I occasionally heard people mention the words "Independence", and "Congress", or speak of "Gandhiji" or "Bapu" with reverence, but I had no clue what these were, or why they should be reason to make anyone, or me in particular, happy or excited.

In today's world it's difficult to imagine how a young man of seventeen could be so ignorant, and so isolated. In 1947, however, the lack of awareness at the ground level was primarily due to lack of communication, and any type of widespread broadcasting media. In my particular case, the reasons were more complicated.

By 1947, and by the time this vaguely-defined Independence came our way, I had been living in the tranquil town of Poona for two and a half years. Although I had no way of knowing it at the time, I was also, after many years of subservience amounting almost to slavery, not very far from my own personal independence.

I had no access to books or magazines, and in any case I could barely read. I would occasionally come across a Marathi or sometimes an English newspaper, and, with a little help from the children of the house, stumblingly began to make sense of the words and sentences. This was how I did eventually learn how to read, but in 1947 when I was 17, I was still quite far from being able to comprehend the concepts of which the newspapers wrote. Of course there was no such thing as television. All India Radio had come into existence a few years previously with the mandate to educate, inform, and entertain. In my father's house in Karachi we had a radio set which had been a source of great pleasure to me. Here, however, I was not entitled to gather around and listen to radio broadcasts along with the family, because I was only their servant. I lived at this time in the home of my father's sister. Her husband's family were traditional moneylenders of our community, and had settled in Poona since the nineteenth century.

Although this was my aunt's family, I had been sent from Karachi to live with them with my role as a domestic employee clearly defined. The family provided me boarding and lodging, and a monthly wage of Rs. 30 which was kept aside to send to my mother and brothers. The pressure of economic need and the hardship of routine daily jobs left little room for family affection or tolerance.

By the time I arrived in Poona, I had become accustomed to this type of life, having worked in a series of tedious, or menial, or difficult jobs ever since my father died on the 5th of June 1942.

Like any other child in our country in those days who had suddenly lost the protection and security of a father's love, guidance, social status and wealth, it was necessary for me to earn my keep, and to be constantly aware that I was obligated to others who had assumed responsibility for me out of a sense of duty. Since their own lives were a struggle, I had to remain silent, obedient, and perform the duties assigned to me to the best of my abilities.

I had become accustomed to this life, but never felt reconciled to it. My mind was constantly wrestling with the thought of how I could get myself out of this wretched situation. I had been loved, respected and surrounded by lavish comfort. How had this happened to me? What was it that had thrust me into this position? Why did I have to endure this type of life, where subjugation and humiliation were a constant backdrop? What could I do to bring myself out of it, assert myself, and seek my own fortune?

In my loneliness, I would look out at the sky and question it. Wherever I was, I would seek the sky – while walking, while sitting, while working, through windows, through the trees – and I would ask, "Why has this happened to me? Why have I been chosen to bear this?"

I was born in Karachi on the 12th of March 1930, into the family of a prosperous businessman. I was named Pahlaj, but everyone called me Palu. My father, Parsram Hukmichand Chhabria, was a prominent member of the wealthy Shikarpuri community. He had a wholesale cloth agency, and one of his major accounts was the sole agency of Messrs Ralli Brothers of U.K. Besides business interests in textiles, my father was also a keen investor in property and in speculative commodities market.

We were ten children, five boys and five girls, and I was the fifth, the one right in the middle. We lived in a huge bungalow with many rooms in what is now called the Gandhi Garden area, one of the most prestigious localities of Karachi.

Wide lawns with flower beds and tall trees surrounded our property. We had our own horse carriage, and a large staff of servants who cared for us children, cooked, cleaned, and ran all the domestic errands. They played with us or accompanied us to the temple in the evenings, tended the horses, and drove the buggy when we went out.

When I was about six or seven, my father decided that we must move to a place which was not so isolated. Our house was situated outside the city. For people who lived in Karachi, a trip to Government Garden or Rani Bagh as it was then called, was an excursion or picnic.

However, it was not a convenient area to live in because for every little thing we needed, someone would have to be sent a long distance to bring it. With so many of us children, it was difficult for my mother. One day I remember, a snake was found in the garden, and this made the decision final because we were used to running around barefoot.

There was a locality called Burns Road being developed in Karachi, and my father bought one of the new buildings there. Along with our family, there were many others, friends, acquaintances and distant relatives, whom my father had given shelter in our bungalow. They had requested him for accommodation, and since we had several unused apartments, he had invited them to stay without rent or expectation of any kind of return. All these people also moved along with us, and we accommodated them in three-bedroom apartments in our building. It was three storeys high, and one of the tall and stately buildings of Karachi at that time.

We lived here for a few years, and I started attending school, in which, to be frank, I was not much interested. Today, children are packed off to school at age three but in our days they were treated differently, and were allowed to run and play as they wished until the age of seven and only then did their schooling begin. It was a Sindhi Medium school – all quite leisurely, and I don't remember there being a fixed time to arrive or leave. By the time I got up and got ready to go to school, playing all the way, it would be 9.30 or 10 a.m. and the other children would have already been there for some time. I would leave by four in the evening. On many days I didn't go to school because I just didn't feel like it, but preferred to play with my friends. The teachers did not bother me much. They knew of my father's wealth and position, and probably wondered what I was doing there in the first place. It was not considered necessary for a child from a successful business family to acquire an education. Usually only those destined for government service, or families of doctors and teachers, would send their children to school. I don't remember ever sitting down to study, or doing homework.

When my father inquired, the teachers complained of my lack of interest, but I confessed to him that I did not like school and would much rather spend my time playing marbles or gulli-danda or flying kites instead.

My memories of my father are dim, because we did not see much of him. He had a large social circle, and his social and professional activities kept him extremely busy. During the day he would sit, firm and upright at his pedhi, impressive-looking in his large yellow pugdi and crisply starched dhoti which he wore with a long white coat. Passers-by would stop to give him a respectful salaam. He was a little stout, and around 5'8" in height. In the evening he would ride out in his buggy to the club or a social function. We children were a little afraid of him and kept our distance.

My mother, Parvati Chhabria, was always at home, but what with ten of us and a large household to manage, she was always busy. She was extremely loving and cared for us all equally. She never showed any favouritism, but I did get the feeling that she was especially fond of me. Perhaps she gave that feeling to each of the others as well, as good mothers often do. She was a quiet, pious woman and spent her time supervising the servants' duties, looking after us children, and reading the Guru Granth Sahib and the Gita in Gurmukhi.

One of my earliest memories is of Sunday afternoons when my father had his siesta. We had an old 78 rpm gramophone, and I would be given the important responsibility of keeping it wound up so that there was no break in the music. One after the other, the soothing voices of K. L. Saigal and Pankaj Mullick and the other soul-stirring Hindi melodies would float into the still afternoon air.

I loved these songs and without any conscious effort seemed to know them all by heart. The other children would often ask me to sing for them, and would be amazed at how I remembered the words and sang with the exact tune and pronunciation.

I spent most of my time playing by myself. One of my few good friends was Thakur Nagdev. Our families were close to each other – we were from the same community, and had a similar social status. Thakur and I were of the same age but attended different schools. His elder sister and my sister Daya were close friends. The family ran the firm Sevaram Sugnomal which was a cloth agency similar to my father's. Based in Karachi, they also had an office in Bombay.

By now World War II had begun making an impact on our shores and it was feared that Karachi would be the target of bomb attacks. Some time towards the end of 1940, my father decided to move the family to safety away from Karachi. We shifted to our ancestral haveli in Shikarpur. It was a beautiful old wooden building with a wide veranda running around the entire inner periphery. A series of rooms led off this veranda. There was a large wooden door at the entrance of the house through which people could come and go freely all day, and it would be locked shut only at night.

Shikarpur District was reputed throughout India for its education and other civic amenities including well-known hospitals and colleges. The famous Sukkur Barrage was just a few miles north of Shikarpur. Built by the British and originally named the Lloyd Barrage, it fed the largest irrigation system in the world, protecting Sindh from the Thar Desert and turning it into a fertile garden with lush fields of wheat, cotton, and sugarcane. Closely linked with India's mythology as well as history, the river Sindhu flowed nearby. With clear blue water, and large, smooth round stones casually decorating its banks, it was said that "It roared and spread itself, but it never hurt." The Sindhu river, the river from which our subcontinent derives its name, signified power, strength, and permanence of the Indian civilization.

Shikarpur had been founded in 1617 as a hunting resort. As towns further south declined, it became popular on the caravan route. This gave the Shikarpuris growing control on the trade between India and central Asia, and the merchant bankers of our community with their indigenous banking system exerted influence as far away as Russia. Towards the end of the nineteenth century, Shikarpuri traders had even begun to establish a hold on the markets of the Middle East.

I loved Shikarpur. Some years previously, my father had sent me there for a holiday with my grandmother. I had friends there, and we spent all our time playing and flying kites. Everyone was very kind, and I enjoyed myself very much.

My grandmother Rukmani Chhabria would have been fifty five or maybe sixty years old, and she seemed impossibly ancient to me. My affectionate nickname for her was Budhiya Bhabhi. In Shikarpur the summers were extremely hot, and the winters extremely cold. I would wake up early and run to my grandmother expecting to be fed. But she would smile and pinch my cheek and push me away to have my bath first. Though I knew this was expected of me, I never failed to try my luck at getting breakfast before I'd had my bath, but she never relented.

In a frenzy of impatience with this cruel grandmother, I would race to the well to draw water for my bath. The buckets we used in those days were large pouches made of jute. The water was freezing cold and naturally leaked copiously out of the jute fibre, splashing my legs as I ran to the outhouse carrying it. Only after my Budhiya Bhabhi was satisfied that I had purified myself adequately for my meal would she start making my chapattis.

When the chapattis were ready, she would have to feed the first one to the fire. The next one had to be fed to the cow. Only then was it my turn! These rituals were extremely significant. They were an important part of the way of life our people had lived for generations together. However, at that moment they were a terrible nuisance to me and by now I would not only be very hungry but also very angry! It annoyed me greatly that she didn't seem in any hurry at all!

One day I went shopping with my grandmother. We walked about fifteen or twenty minutes from home to buy groceries and sweetmeats.

Of the many sweet shops in Shikarpur, there was one which we favoured the most. It was always crowded, and I once asked my grandmother why we couldn't go to another less crowded shop, tugging her arm and trying to pull her into one which looked exactly the same to me but without any other customers. No, she explained, we would only shop at the best place, where the freshest, best quality ingredients were used, where they understood the dynamics of taste, and where customers were honoured as if they were kings. "That's why his shop is more crowded than the others!" she smiled at me, "Everyone wants the best!"

Buying sweets was one of my most favourite activities. A smiling, pot-bellied man dressed in a white kurta and dhoti would welcome us into the shop. We would push our way into the haven of delight and seat ourselves on low wooden benches in front of him. There were mounds and layers of sweets of different types stacked all around us. There would be many people waiting to select the delicacies, and the smiling shopkeeper would serve us all as rapidly as he could. He would begin to offer samples, and on to me fell the agreeable task of tasting each one and choosing those that I found most delicious. I would get to work at once in a stupor of happiness, my grandmother watching me with a fond smile on her face, until I could eat no more.

On the way back from this pleasant expedition that day, I started dragging my feet and my grandmother went ahead. I soon realised that I did not know where I was. In those days, Shikarpur had a bazaar with covered streets, somewhat like the covered bazaars of Bukhara, Samarkand and Istanbul. The long and narrow market was lined with shops on both sides and passed through the entire length of the city. To my dismay, all the havelis looked the same! Each one had shops and stalls outside the entrance, and they all looked identical. I looked around me and my Budhiya Bhabhi was nowhere to be seen. I realised that I was lost, and started running, crying, trying to look into each haveli, completely confused and in a panic. Finally, I saw something that looked a little familiar and peeped inside, and what sweet relief I felt to find myself at home! Ever since that day it has been my habit to pay close attention to my surroundings no matter where I am.

My favourite pastime was to fly kites and I would be up on the terrace no matter how sunny it got, and stay up there until my grandmother had begun firing the kerosene lamps after the sun went down. They would shout for me to come down, but in vain! The old havelis were all quite close to each other and I remember one day when my kite got stuck on a high balcony of the neighbouring building. I climbed down the side of our house, jumped across, and climbed onto the next house without a second thought to rescue my kite.

These days when I read about children in crowded cities like Ahmedabad who accidentally fall off their terraces in pursuit of their kites, I remember that carefree moment of my childhood when nothing, not even my life, was more important than a kite! It was a particularly blissful phase, with never a thought for consequences.

When I returned to Karachi after several weeks in this paradise, I had lost my taste for school even further. I would skip school as often as possible, and run out to play in the morning, but would make sure I came rushing home early to have my dinner so that I would be fast asleep before my father returned. That way I was able to avoid any scolding or difficult questions from him!

I also loved exploring. My friends and I would often go out on our bicycles and visit different parts of the city, sometimes quite far away. When I came home late in the evening and was asked where I had been all day, I would casually say that I had been playing at my friend's house.

If I had only known what an advantage a little education would have been to me in the years to come! Today when I think with regret of those days, I have no one to blame but myself.

By the time my father decided to move us safely away from the threat of bombs in Karachi to Shikarpur, he had modernised the haveli a little and had even got our home electrified.

Our eldest sister Daya had got married in 1943, into the Ahuja family who had business interests in Bombay, Calcutta, and Amritsar. She and her husband Bhajandas were now settled in Amritsar.

9

Bhagwandas, the eldest brother and eight years senior to me, remained in Karachi with our father. He was being groomed to take over the family business. The rest of us, along with our mother, now moved to Shikarpur to live in the haveli with our grandmother. Ramchand, four years older than me, had also begun to learn the ropes of my father's business in Karachi. However, since he was recovering from a childhood illness and was still weak, he spent most of his time with us in Shikarpur. My sister Kaushalya was older than me, but the others, Laxmi, Kishan, Indira, Shanti and Narayan, were younger. Here too, we had many servants. It was a life of comfort and peace.

Then one fateful day in June 1942 the family received a telegram which brought news that changed our lives forever.

A telegram invariably meant bad tidings. As it was in English, someone had to be called to read it out. Hearts beating fast, the family members present in the house at the time listened in dreaded anticipation. But the news was even worse than the worst any of them could have imagined. My father was no more. He had succumbed to a massive heart attack.

A messenger was sent to fetch me from school. I remember the class in which we sat on the floor, balancing our slates on our lap. The teacher stood in front, writing something on the board. Even at that age, I found it more attractive to look out of the window and gaze at the sky. I was just twelve years old and had been in school for less than five years.

That day, they came and took me away from school and I never saw the inside of a classroom again.

We continued to live in Shikarpur for some months but after the period of mourning had ended, we returned to Karachi. To our great surprise, the home we were taken to in Karachi was not the spacious place of comfort we had previously known. Instead, it was a tiny rented flat with two and a half bedrooms. The servants were all gone. At first I thought that we had moved because it would be unbearable for us to live in the place where my father had died.

However, it soon became clear that it wasn't just our residence that had changed, but our entire standard of living. There was no money to run the house. Overnight, we had lost everything.

All the property, bank accounts, and my father's investments had been transferred to my mother's name. Over the next few days, my brothers asked for her signature on various documents, and everything was given away. My mother was also told to hand over most of her gold jewellery. Already traumatised by the loss of our father, these events were a further shock. I had no idea what had happened, but my elder brothers were now in charge. I would never have dreamt of confronting them or even meekly asking for an explanation. At that time I was too young to do so, but even if I had been older, it would not have been possible. Elders were obeyed out of sheer convention and it was not possible to argue or question. Our relationship had clear-cut boundaries, and though the bonds were extremely strong, we tended to be formal and reserved with each other. Frank and direct communication was not possible.

It was many years before I learnt the truth. At that time, I only overheard murmurs of what had happened. World War II had given rise to speculation in the commodities market. Many merchants had multiplied their fortunes in a short period by trading in cotton and other products. My brothers had money, property and other investments. However, they had neither experience nor reliable advisors. During the time between the death of my father and our return to Karachi, their speculation had resulted in losses of a higher value than our entire assets. Stunned by this turn of events, and ashamed of what they had done, they liquidated everything, and repaid all the debts.

I heard others in the community whisper that they had taken these actions to honour our father's name. These whispers must have been especially painful to my mother, but her pride in their actions gave her the strength to remain calm and silent.

In 1942, my brothers were just twenty and sixteen years old. They had neither knowledge of the business world, nor skills of negotiation, nor personal vision. They were suffering terribly because of the sudden loss of our father. However, the one thing that stood by them was the strong sense of family honour, something they had inherited from the previous generations. Finding themselves in debt, they had divested themselves of the entire family property, wealth, possessions, heirlooms and jewellery to make the necessary repayment. They did not consider holding anything back with the purpose of preserving even a little of our comfort or independence.

It did not matter that by doing this they were leaving their mother and their young brothers and sisters homeless and in a pitiably vulnerable and unprotected condition. What mattered was that no one would ever have a reason to call us cheats or consider us dishonourable in any way. I was unable to understand why things had changed so suddenly. All I knew was that I was uncomfortable and unhappy, and that somehow they were to blame. It took many years for my resentment to transform into appreciation.

My mother, already devastated at being left widowed, took this further blow in her stride. She had been born in Quetta and had come to Karachi when she married my father. She used to tell us about how she had lost her own father and two elder brothers in an earthquake at about the time when I was born. My father had no brothers, and his one surviving sister lived far away in Poona. She now had no one to whom we could turn for advice or support. There was no other family on whom we could rely.

My mother's life experiences had taught her that existence was unpredictable, and given her an inner resilience. She mourned briefly, and turned quietly to immerse herself in her new duties. The servants were gone, and all the housework fell to her and my sisters. With Daya already married, there were now nine of us children at home. Some were still very young. My grandmother visited us in Karachi as often as she could. I loved her and was happy. But for my mother it was a time not just of sorrow but of the exhaustion brought on by sheer labour.

Bhagwandas had resourcefully managed to continue our father's business with the Ralli agency. Forerunner of the Indian pharmaceutical and agriculture products Tata company Rallis India, Ralli Brothers was the London-based concern of Greek Ralli brothers, one of the most successful expatriate merchant businesses of the Victorian era. Trading in jute, shellac, sesame seed, turmeric, ginger, rice, saltpetre and borax, they had offices in Calcutta and Bombay and employed around 4000

12

clerks and 15000 warehousemen and dockers in India, and brought prized products from the mills of Manchester into India. So strong was the brand built by Ralli Brothers that in our areas the name was synonymous with fabric. Till today, the traditional patchwork, appliquéd and embroidered quilts indigenous to the area with designs inherited from mother to daughter since time immemorial and internationally coveted, go by the name of Ralli quilts.

Ramchand had acquired a position with Mulchand Chandrabhan & Co. at a salary of Rs. 60 per month. This company had clients from Afghanistan who sold produce of the region such as dry fruit and nuts, and they had clients in Karachi who bought these items. Their business was to broker successful transactions and earn their commission from both parties. Ramchand was now sent to Afghanistan, and later to Bombay.

As for me, it was well known that I was not interested in school and had not learnt much in the years I had been attending. With the family in need of money, it was no longer possible for me to lead a life of leisure! It was decided that I would have to make myself useful and go to work. Our family was well connected in the cloth trade, and it was easy for my brothers to find me a job in a cloth shop even though I was not yet thirteen years old.

So it was that my employment history began with a position in the wholesale cloth shop of Ramchand Brothers in Karachi, with a salary package of Rs. 10 per month.

As a worker, I had to change my style of dress from the shirt and shorts I had worn all these years and adopt the more grown-up kurta-pajama and topi. Since I could barely read or write, I could be given only casual work. My duties included sweeping and cleaning the shop before we started the day, offering water to customers, clearing away the samples of fabric and other goods after they left, and performing any odd job I was given.

All this was a great shock for me. My childhood had led me to believe that work was something done only by servants. If I ever needed something, there was always someone who would rush to bring it or do it for me.

I had never even helped myself to a single glass of water. We employed someone whose duty it was to help me have a bath. Until the death of my father when I was twelve, I had never dressed myself without help. It was just incomprehensible that I should now find myself in this position.

My work day started at about 10.30 each morning, and went on till 9 at night. It was a small shop, with thick cotton gaddis on the floor on which customers could sit and view and examine samples of cloth from the various mills, comparing their merits of colour, design and texture. They were mostly villagers who had come to Karachi to buy bundles of fabric which they would carry back and sell in the villages to make shirts and dhotis. Wealthy customers, or those known to my employers, would be offered sharbat or lassi. In Sindh in those days, tea and coffee had not yet gained popularity. To offer a drink, I would have to look down, my body bent in a submissive attitude, and hold the tray out, offering it hesitantly. I learnt to shrink away and be invisible until I was called for. I realise now that if at all I was able to do a good job during that time, it was only because I must have subconsciously observed the serving attitude of the staff we had in our home. It was very painful, especially because I had always been used to having things my own way. This was my first experience of being dominated, and I was given no choice but to develop the skills of compliance and obedience.

It was considered unthinkable that a servant should sit in the presence of the employers. I would have to stand all day in a corner of the shop. At noon, the sethji would send me to his home to fetch his lunch. I would serve him and wash up after he had finished. I could then eat my meal, which would comprise the few chapattis my mother had packed for me in the morning. Sometimes the sethji's wife would offer me leftovers from her kitchen.

In today's world washing dishes after a meal is quite common and even those who are used to having servants would have had the experience, perhaps during phases of visiting or living in other countries if not at home. But for a child with my upbringing to have to wash vessels, especially those used by others, was extremely degrading.

By the time I returned to the crowded uncomfortable place I could not yet accept as my home, I would be exhausted. My mind was in a constant state of turmoil. Why had I been picked out and sent to do this demeaning work? I yearned for my earlier life of luxury and position. There was no one I could talk to about my thoughts and feelings. My friend Thakur came looking for me occasionally and would sometimes press me to go out with him in his family's car. Though I had a weekly off as well as a holiday on the day preceding the night of the new moon, I was so ashamed of my new status that, though I appreciated his kindness and affection, I tried to avoid him and the others I had spent time with in happier days. Most of the other children I had been friendly with kept away from me.

I continued with this job for six months, and then my brothers found me another similar position at double the salary. It was ironic that my first two employers shared names with my two elder brothers. Now for Rs. 20 per month I was employed by the cloth merchants Bhagwandas Makhija. The only difference here was that the shop was larger.

One day as I was walking home, glancing up from time to time to ask the sky, "Why! Why!!" I heard my name called out.

I looked up and saw someone gesturing to me from the upper window of a building I had been walking past. It was Somnath, who had been a cook with our family for many years. Somnath had taken great care of me when I was younger. He would feed me and tell me stories from Tehri Garhwal where his family was, and where he had lived as a child. We had been very fond of each other.

When we had lost our family wealth, all our staff had been relieved of their duties and I had assumed that Somnath must have gone back to his beloved village. Immersed in my daily misery, I had not given him a thought. At first I was embarrassed that he should see me in this condition, but he called out to me so insistently, and with so much affection, that I went.

I was surprised to see that Somnath was now running his own eating establishment, a kind of canteen in the cloth market. The concept of a restaurant was not yet popular with the common people of Sindh, but

Somnath and others like him ran kitchens which provided a meal service for travellers, or bachelors living on their own for a monthly fee. He hugged me, and wept seeing what had become of me. After inquiring after all the family members, he sat me on his lap and began ordering his workers to bring choice delicacies and sweets which he knew I loved. He fed me with his own hands.

I had mixed feelings about this reunion. The thought that never left me was that Somnath, who once had been a servant in my home and to my young mind had lived just to do my bidding, was now the master of his own establishment with servants of his own. I realised, as never before, that unplanned events would occur without any warning and life would keep changing. I understood that I should never be complacent about any situation I was in. And similarly I understood that though my position at present seemed so hopeless, I must not despair because it would continue to change. No one could tell what tomorrow would bring! I resolved to never rest and to live my life always looking and moving ahead, and doing everything within my power to change all that needed to be changed.

After a short stint with Bhagwandas Makhija, I moved on to another similar job, but due to irregular supply of cloth, the shop was closed down. After this I was employed for a brief period in the hosiery shop of a Bohri Muslim family at Sadar Bazaar. I had to walk several miles to get to this shop. The owners lived above it, and they had a habit of entering silently to check on me. If by chance they found me sitting idle, they would purposely scatter material around and insist that either I or the other boy working there should clean it thoroughly and replace everything very carefully.

This particular humiliation was just too much to bear. My family felt my misery deeply, and my brothers now found work for me with Wadhuram Chhabria, a building contractor who was a distant relative.

Wadhuram had three second-hand army trucks which carried stone and sand from the quarry and various other materials to and from the government projects that had been allotted to him. It was wartime, petrol was a scarce commodity. Since vehicle petrol tanks were easy to open, pilferage was common. My job was to travel in the trucks and keep an eye on the drivers and make sure that no petrol was stolen.

To get to the Wadhuram office, I had to walk some three or four kilometres every morning. We would get into the truck by about 9.30 or 10.00 o'clock and set off. By the time we got back and the driver parked the truck and returned the key to the office, it would be night, sometimes 8 or 9 o'clock, or even as late as 10. The trucks were large, noisy old vehicles in very poor condition, and they bumped and lurched violently on the roads to and from the quarry. When I got home at night I would be exhausted, and would drop off into a deep sleep, only to wake up and set off again early next morning. Day after day, the routine was tedious and I found the hours passing by without any meaning.

It was hot and uncomfortable in the cabin of the truck and as we rode along, I would stare out of the window at the sky and continue to question it. Why did I have to do this? What had happened to the life I used to live? Often, I began to sing one of the old Saigal melodies that my father had loved so much, and forgot where I was or what I was doing.

The drivers of the fleet were all Pathans. In Sindh in those days, there were many different ethnic minorities.

These Pushto-speaking tribal people hailed from Afghanistan and the North West Frontier Province of what later became Pakistan. Pathans had a reputation for enterprise, bravery, and hospitality. However, the Pathan stereotype also included such characteristics as envy, obstinacy, and a tendency to seek revenge. Pathans are usually tall and big built, with strong, sharp features and light eyes. Most of them used the surname Khan. They wore their traditional baggy salwar and loose kurta with pockets. From a Pathan's head-dress, which ranged from an elaborate pugdi to embroidered wool caps, you could tell exactly which tribe he represented.

Many feared the Pathans, but they were very friendly to me. At the office my sad plight and my father's reputation were well known and the lorry drivers treated me with kindness and respect. When they stopped at roadside dhabas for rest and refreshments, they would share their lassi or glass of milk, and sometimes even offer me a snack. They were easy to get along with and I was soon able to converse with them in Pushto.

Sometime in early 1944, Bhagwandas took me to Amritsar. Daya's husband, Bhajandas Chainrai Ahuja, had offered that I could live with them and help him in his business.

I had now been working for nearly two years and had acquired a good amount of experience. My brother-in-law knew I could be relied on. They ran a wholesale cloth trade, buying goods from Bombay and supplying them to various small retailers in Amritsar. He assigned me the duty of collecting money from these customers.

By and large, I found this duty to be tiring, but not particularly difficult. I would set off in the morning with a list of shops to be visited and details of the dues from each one, and walk from one to the other, collecting money. I was only 14 years old, still a child. Most of the Punjabi shopkeepers from whom I had to ask for payment were, by contrast, burly men with loud voices and an aggressive manner. Yet, I was always treated with courtesy. Perhaps this was because of my calm appearance, or maybe it had something to do with my name.

I had been called Palu at home but now they started calling me Kalu, and then someone added Shah, perhaps as an endearment or as a title, and when I entered a shop and announced that I was Kalushah, the name got an immediate response and I would be courteously asked to sit. If there were other creditors waiting, I would often be given preference for payment. If they were unable to pay at that moment, they would politely request me to come again.

At the end of the day, I was expected to note down the collection particulars – which shops I had visited, and how much I had been given at each place. This was my first introduction to the written word, writing accounts in Sindhi. I was not very good at it, but it was now that I first learnt to communicate by writing.

This life was an improvement over the drudgery I had suffered in Karachi. It was also the first time I had been out of Sindh. Though the people, the language, and the food were quite different to what I had been used to, I found Amritsar an interesting place, somewhat similar to Shikarpur with old buildings, narrow roads, and crowded bazaars in which the shops were so close that you could even shout across from one to the other. The people were extremely friendly and helpful. I soon found myself conversing in the local language without any apparent effort. In the course of my work the people I dealt with were mostly elderly Sikhs. I found them always kind and affectionate towards me, providing me with valuable guidance, from which I learnt a lot. My life was challenging, but I now found it quite interesting too.

I was lucky that we lived close to the Golden Temple. After work every evening, I would climb up to the terrace and look out at it. In summer the heat indoors would be stifling and we would sleep on the terrace. The gentle chant of satsang or gurbani could be heard at all times, and I found it very soothing. It was the same sky overhead that had followed me wherever I went and I would look up and ask, "What am I doing here?" and think about the life I used to lead, the jobs I had worked at in Karachi, and wonder what was going to happen after this.

I had the day off on Sunday, which I made use of in my favourite pastime of exploring the city. I was already familiar with most of the roads and areas because of my work, and I always found it interesting to observe the different activities I saw. I remember once going with the family in a tonga to visit the gurdwara at Tarntarn.

There were interesting places to visit but when I was tired I always took refuge in the Harmandir Sahib. It is a huge place and I would sit quietly in one corner and watch and listen, and wonder about the world and why things happen the way they do, and always come away with a beautiful, calm feeling inside.

By the end of 1944, however, I had to leave Amritsar. The supplies of cloth had been erratic and then they stopped. My brother-in-law had to close down the business. It was decided that I should be sent back to Karachi.

Though I was only 14, I was no longer treated as a child. It was an overnight journey of 36 hours from Amritsar to Karachi, and I would have to change trains at Lahore, but nobody thought I was too young to travel alone. I had been a working person for a long time and it never occurred to me either. I had already learnt how to hold my own with all kinds of people. The experiences at the different shops in Karachi, the truck journeys with the Pathans and my life as a collection agent wandering around the by-lanes of Amritsar on my own had given me some maturity. It was of no great concern that I would be going on a long overnight journey where I would have no one to help me change trains.

Daya had just had a baby, a lovely little girl, and was unable to accompany us to the station. My brother-in-law bought me a ticket, gave me a few annas to take care of myself on the journey, and saw me off. As we were parting, he presented me with a ten-rupee note.

Ten rupees was an enormous sum of money, and the ten-rupee note was a much larger, flapping version of the one we use today. Owning this note made me extraordinarily proud. In those days you could buy a bicycle for ten rupees. The ticket from Amritsar to Karachi via Lahore cost only three rupees.

I had been earning money for a long time, but all of it had been given to my brothers. They were running the house, they were responsible for me, and it was given to them as their due, without any question. All my employers would pay them directly, and I never knew or asked what became of it. Even now, the entire sum that I had earned in the last one year would be sent to them. This was the first time I had ever seen and held my own money!

During the past year I had become used to collecting large sums of money from the various shopkeepers my brother-in-law supplied to. Now, for the very first time, this ten rupees was my own. I rolled up the huge note and tucked it away safely into my kurta pocket, but I could not stop myself from taking it out repeatedly and staring at it. Delighted with my new wealth, excited at the journey ahead of me and at the thought of going home again, I waved goodbye to my brother-in-law as the train slowly left the platform.

I settled myself on the wooden seat in the third-class compartment of the Lahore train, pleasantly surprised to see that I had a Pathan for my neighbour. He in turn was amused to discover my fluency in Pushto, and we chatted for a while. When he dozed off, I began to hum and sing to myself, lost in the melody and only coming out of my reverie to smile when others in the compartment called out their appreciation of my song.

I continued taking out my lovely ten-rupee note at intervals and admiring it. I gazed with appreciation at its colours and designs and numbers. As evening fell, I took the precaution of curling the giant note up carefully and slipping it in with my pyjama nada. When I climbed onto a little wooden window shelf to pass the night, I slept peacefully knowing that my precious note was safe.

Next morning the train stopped at Larkana station. I woke excitedly. Though we were still some hours away from home, we were back in Sindh, my homeland. I leaned out of the train window, revelling in the sights, sounds and smells, delighted to hear my native language shouted across the platform. I had been away from this familiar and soothing environment for many months and had not realised how much I had missed it or the specific feelings it drew forth, and how much it meant to me. Perhaps it's just as well that I didn't realise then that these sights and sounds and smells would soon be lost to me forever, and that the feeling of connectedness, of coming home to your motherland, was something that would very soon be snatched away from me, never to be returned.

I leaped out onto the platform, looking forward to the hot puri-bhaji and tall glass of hot, sweet milk that awaited. I reached in to take my ten-rupee note out of its secret hiding place. What a shock I got when I realised that it was gone!

I began frantically searching for it, just in case I had absentmindedly put it somewhere else, digging deep into my pockets and shaking out my clothes, hoping against hope that it would turn up. After a few moments I knew that I had to face the fact that it was lost. I was aware of the Pathan watching me quietly and I asked him if he knew where my note was. He quickly shrugged his shoulders, indicating that he did not.

I took my courage in my hands and ran out onto the platform, shouting, "Alarum! Alarum!" Hearing my cries, the message quickly spread down the station and the ticket collector arrived.

Things were different in those days. The railway officials were courteous, well-spoken people. They had time for you, and they were there to help you, even if you happened to be only a fourteen-year-old who had lost the largest sum of money he had ever owned.

It was time for us to start moving again, but with an important case like this on hand, the ticket collector had the power to delay the train. He climbed in to inspect the scene where the money had been lost. He questioned me in detail, and finally informed me that there was absolutely no chance that I would get the money back. "There are so many people in this carriage," he said. "Each and every one of them could be carrying a ten-rupee note! Even if I was to search them all, how would we know which one was yours?"

Hearing this, I now jumped up with excitement. "We will know!" I shouted triumphantly, "I can tell you the number on my note!"

I had spent so much time admiring and staring at my note in fascination that I could now remember every digit of the number on it. Polite but disbelieving, the ticket collector wrote down the number I told him. He then kindly asked me if I suspected any of my co-passengers in particular. I replied at once that it had to be the Pathan. There was absolutely no doubt whatever in my mind that he was the one who had taken it. We had spent time talking, and he had seen the note very clearly. He had been right next to me and I had been fast asleep all night. The Pathan was questioned, but he denied knowledge of any ten-rupee note.

It is many years since I remembered this incident but when I think about it now, I feel surprised at the simple assurance I had shown that day. Sure enough, when the Pathan was searched, the note was found in his pugdi. When the number was checked, it was exactly the same as the one I had given the ticket collector.

To my great surprise and frustration, it was now not a simple matter of retrieving my note and completing the short journey home. There were official procedures to be carried out. The train had been delayed long enough, and we were asked to climb out so that it could move on. It was early in the morning and we stepped onto the platform with our bags and bundles.

I did not have to worry about informing my family members of this change in plan. The truth is that though they must have received some communication that I was on my way, they could not have known when exactly to expect me. In those days, when people went on a journey or a pilgrimage, you could be sure of their arrival only after you saw them. The ticket collector escorted us to the railway police station and handed over our case. A punchnama, the First Information Report or FIR, the formal documentation of the event, was made out. The police recorded the Pathan's thumb print. We now had to wait till 11 o'clock when the court opened.

At the Larkana court house, I was informed to my surprise that I would have to appoint a lawyer to represent my case. Here was something new! There were a few gentlemen in black gowns standing outside, and I approached one of them, but was dismayed to find he was expecting five rupees for his services! For a moment I considered walking back to the station and catching the next train to Karachi. I did have a valid ticket in my pocket, after all. But then I thought, why should I give up all rights to my hard earned money? If these were the laws of our land, then I knew I should abide by them. I would also do all I could to retrieve what was mine. So I negotiated a fee of three rupees, and waited for my name to be called.

The court was a calm and rather dignified place. Ours was the only case up for hearing, and it was quite straightforward. The missing goods had been recovered. The culprit had confessed, and in fact had now begun wailing loudly, begging sympathy and forgiveness, no doubt less from any genuine remorse than fear of the punishment that lay in store!

I finally reached home late that evening to a joyous welcome from my mother. After paying the lawyer's fee and all the other expenses of the journey, I now had hardly six rupees left in my pocket.

More than anything else, this incident taught me to trust my judgement. Laying aside my shock at losing the money I had been able to see very simply that the Pathan was the most likely suspect. I had had within me the boldness to call the authorities. Ever since that day, I have always had complete faith in my common sense and instinct. They have very rarely let me down.

2

Lakshmi Road, Poona, 1945

INDEPENDENCE

"I had worked in sales situations for long enough to know how to make a customer feel important. If someone got particularly annoyed at my persistence and ordered me to leave, I would do so, and simply wait for a few days before going back and quietly trying again. I never allowed the feeling of rejection to influence my next action, but kept calmly focussed on my objective instead."

When I first saw Bombay, I felt disappointed.

In 1945, Karachi was one of India's most modern cities. What had been a sleepy town of just 15,000 inhabitants in 1843 was developed by the British into one of the most modern towns in India, and the largest grain-exporting port of their empire. It had wide new roads and impressive buildings. Karachi had an aerodrome in the early 1930s, even before the one at Bombay was built. Our city was one of only five in the country through which trams ran, providing safe and efficient public transport.

Sindh did not suffer from a rigid caste system or the atrocities of caste-based practice common to some parts of the country, but most Indian communities did have traditional occupations that they practised. Even the modern occupations tended to attract those from the same community, just as truck drivers were invariably Pathans. The many Parsi families in the city engaged in business and industry, and they were also responsible for a large number of institutions such as schools

and hospitals. Amongst us Shikarpuris, trading and money-lending businesses had been handed down over the generations, and it was normal to spend the entire day sitting in one's shop. There was very little physical activity, and the concept of exercising to stay fit was unknown. Diabetes and heart disease were common, but we were not aware that they were a result of this sedentary lifestyle.

When I visited Karachi as a member of the SAARC[1] committee through FICCI[2] in 1994, I was shocked and disappointed to see the city in what appeared to me a state of ruin. Gone were the stately old bungalows with their red tiles and deep verandas enclosed by latticed window screens. I was unable to locate my home or any familiar building or locality. It was totally unlike the Karachi I had known, and was in even worse disarray than Mumbai is today.

In my memory, Karachi was a beautiful, well-designed city surrounded by plantations of sugar, cotton, and wheat. The city itself had many gardens and parks, schools, colleges, and hospitals; stately and elegant. Life was leisurely spent, people were content, and the markets overflowed with fresh vegetables from the nearby countryside, and fruit from Chaman. Almonds, Pistachios, and Dates were freely available and inexpensive. Our meals were simple and consisted of dal, vegetables and chapattis. On special occasions, traditional sweets would be prepared. In our family, and for Shikarpuris in general, sweets are a great favourite. Karachi being a coastal city, the temperatures were never extreme, unlike Larkana, Shikarpur and Sukkur which suffered extremes of both heat and cold. We enjoyed a mild monsoon in the months from June to September, and our city with its natural harbour was protected from storms by surrounding islands.

It was a day in 1945 when I arrived from Karachi at the Bombay Central railway station. Greeted by noise, dirt and crowds, and a level of disorder that seemed to me far inferior to the peace and stateliness of the Karachi roads, I stepped back in distaste. My memory fails me regarding the exact month, but it was the middle of the monsoon with torrential rains. In Karachi, rain had been a pleasant occurrence. I had never in my life experienced these blinding sheets of water pelting down and it seemed as if they would never stop.

[1]   South Asian Association for Regional Cooperation
[2]   Federation of Indian Chambers of Commerce and Industry

I somehow made my way to the office of Mulchand Chandrabhan & Co. where I was to stay overnight. I remember being fascinated by their way of doing business. They paid for most of the goods they dealt in not in cash but in an elaborate system of barter, buying tea, spices and various grains for the Pathans who brought them their stock.

Ramchand was away, and I stayed on until he arrived. He lived in Khar, and I found the Bombay local trains and the bustle of Bombay peculiar and unattractive but interesting. After a few days, Ramchand took me to Bombay's historic railway station, the elaborately carved Victoria Terminus and put me on the train to Poona.

The rain followed us in the train as well, drenching the thick green mountainside and even trickling down the sides of the tunnels the train hooted through. These new experiences were a little frightening, even for an experienced 15-year-old traveller like me, but I had come to learn that you can't stop doing what you have to do just because you happen to be apprehensive! As was my habit, I gazed out at the sky as it reappeared at the mouth of the tunnel, and felt my unhappiness lift a little as I shared my thoughts and feelings with it.

There was a new job waiting for me in Poona. My father's sister had married into the family of a Poona money-lender, Harbhagwandas Lachhmandas Sakhrani. They had indicated to my elder brother that they would give me boarding and lodging and a monthly wage of Rs. 30 in return for my services. Three months after my return from Amritsar, I had been told to pack my bags and set off again. My mother and grandmother shed a few tears, but by now I had become quite used to the itinerant lifestyle.

Poona was my first experience of a place where I was not able to communicate easily right from the start. In Sindh, although many languages were spoken, Hindi was always a common link. In the Bohri shop they had spoken Gujarati, but we could communicate in Hindi. The Sindhis, the Pathans, the Punjabis and all the other communities spoke in their own languages, but we could always communicate with one another in Hindi, even if it was just a few broken words. When I arrived in Poona, and tried to hire a tonga to take me to my aunt's home at Lakshmi Road, I soon discovered that the tongawala and I could not understand a word of what the other was saying! Passers-by stopped and helped us out. We had to make signs with our fingers to negotiate the fare.

I remember that day with amusement. In a few months I was able to converse easily in Marathi, and today it is one of the languages in which I am most comfortable. I can barely read my native Sindhi, but can plough through Marathi documents and publications. When I make a speech, I feel more comfortable in Marathi than even English.

My aunt's family lived on the second floor of a small building. A narrow wooden terrace separated two apartments, and one of the rooms facing the terrace had been converted into the place of business. I would start the day by thoroughly cleaning this area. Here too it was a tiny shop with a low bench and mattresses on the floor. Customers would come to borrow money or pay interest on lapsed loans. The relevant documents would be signed and stamped, and money would exchange hands.

In Sindh, tea had not been common, but in Poona no one could live without it. I soon got used to serving chai, carrying it across into the shop for customers from the living quarters. With my history as a collection agent, recovery was added to my list of activities here as well. When someone came in with a large repayment, I would have to take the money and deposit it in the bank. I soon learnt how to fill deposit slips and other bank routines, gradually expanding my skills in documentation.

Banking hours were limited then as they are now, but the day was long, and there was plenty of time for me to do domestic chores. In those days too Poona suffered a water shortage. Municipal water came to the taps in the area where we lived only after 10 p.m. It was my job to stay up at night, filling buckets and other containers with cooking and washing water for the next day. This would take around two hours, so I would get to bed only after midnight. Yet I would have to be up at the crack of dawn to collect milk for the family from the milkman who came by on his bicycle.

I was often sent to buy vegetables. At the market, communication would be largely by way of gestures and single-word questions, asked loudly and hopefully, groping for some medium of communication. I would try out words from the various languages I knew until I got some glimmer of understanding from the vendor.

A newcomer to the city who did not know the local language I was a source of great curiosity. After partition things changed, and the influx of Sindhis and Punjabis brought in the first level of diversity that this city had seen. In 1945, however, when I was still finding my feet in Poona, there would always be a crowd watching when I tried to speak to a local, with many helpful translation suggestions flying back and forth. This way I gradually learnt the language. Since this was the first time in my life I was buying vegetables, at home too I would often find choice words of an unfamiliar language waiting for me and I learnt to deal with those as well. Sometimes helpful women would show me how to select good-quality vegetables. I soon observed how crafty vendors manipulated weights, and learnt to keep an eye on them with great shrewdness!

I was given time off every month, and from 4 to 6.30 p.m. on every fourth Sunday I indulged in my favourite hobby of exploring. My debt-recovery duties had already taken me to all corners of the city, but by riding around on the rented bicycle at leisure I soon became familiar with every landmark and establishment.

Poona had no specific industry or business. It was a city to which people would retire and live a calm, peaceful life. There was also a student population, because the Deccan Education Society, and its many educational institutes set up by our revered freedom fighter Lokmanya Bal Gangadhar Tilak and others, had been active here since the latter part of the nineteenth century.

Poona had no high-rise buildings or apartment blocks. The climate was pleasant throughout the year and hardly any home in Poona had a fan.

I noticed that shopkeepers in Poona led a leisurely life. They raised their shutters at mid-morning and took a three-hour lunch break, reopening after a lengthy siesta. Even while their shops were open, customers were few and far between. It was very different from the bustling scenes I had left behind in Karachi and Amritsar. The shelves were dusty and unattractive, and the shopkeepers not particularly inclined to provide excellent service to their customers.

I observed that Poona was divided into two distinct areas – the city itself in which we lived and the cantonment area which had been built by the British.

To get to Main Street from my home on Lakshmi Road took ten or twelve minutes on my bicycle. Years later Main Street was renamed Mahatma Gandhi Road, and today the distance between the two keeps increasing, separated as they are by the increasing density of people and traffic. In the mid-1940s, however, the population of Poona was as low as 100,000. There were hardly any cars on the wide streets and people rode around mostly in tongas or on bicycles, though an occasional Austin or Ford could be seen. The roads were well maintained and watered every day. Though the Poona drains were uncovered, there would be a daily inspection by the civic authorities. The British were very hygiene-conscious, particularly in this important cantonment town.

From Main Street I would cycle towards the Southern Command, an area I liked very much. It had broad roads lined with beautiful old trees and I would occasionally come across a British soldier riding past on his bicycle, perhaps headed for the shooting range on Golibar Maidan. The Koregaon Park area had bungalows surrounded by large gardens and many trees, and the entire stretch of what is now called Dhole Patil Road was lined with buffalo sheds which supplied milk to various parts of the city.

At that time, shops in the Camp area were still housed in the stately old British buildings, and customers would ride up in their buggies. The Royal Bakery, Poona Drug Stores and Bombay Swadeshi were some of the stores that can still be seen. A major landmark on East Street, the Albert Petit Library, is still in existence though a shell of its former glory. West End and Capitol were plush cinema halls which screened English movies.

There were many open spaces and maidans throughout Poona. Some of these were the Botanical Gardens, the Empress Garden, and the Bund Garden. They would often have a band play there on Saturdays. I loved to go to the Bund Garden in the evenings where people would gather to sit and watch the river flow quietly past. The water was so clear that you could even see the fish in it.

The entire area all the way from Ganesh Khind Road to the Governor's House and Observatory was lined with a profusion of tall flowering trees which towered and formed a beautiful canopy overhead. Cycling on this road, I would occasionally glance up to greet the sky as I loved to do, but see only branches and leaves and flowers, an equally heavenly sight! Small bungalows nestled amongst the trees. The jhopadis came later. Of course there was poverty, but no hutment colonies as yet.

Poona came to life on weekends during the racing season when people from different cities, particularly Bombay, would drive down to their bungalows, to get away from their hectic lives and briefly share our leisure and temperate climate. The railways had a special race-goer's train leaving Bombay early morning, and returning at the end of the racing day. While the races coloured life in the westernized section of Poona, in our native city, where I lived, it was the Ganesh festival that was our single most important annual event. The Sarvajanik Ganeshotsav or community celebration of Ganesh had been introduced by Lokmanya Tilak in 1894 in an effort to challenge the British domination of our culture. It had now become an integral part of life in the city, as it continues to be. Every year people participated with faith and fervour rather than noise and braggadocio, and there was no disruption to city life as there is today.

Most of the locals lived in the old traditional houses known as wadas which were somewhat like our havelis in the north. Families lived clustered together in these old wooden houses. Some of them rented out rooms or apartments. There would be one large main door, which could be bolted shut at night. A lot of the pensioners had built bungalows with gardens to enjoy their retirement. The city clustered around the old communities or Peths of Kasbapeth, Sadashivpeth, Narayanpeth, Budhwarpeth, Somwarpeth, and Rastapeth. The Deccan Gymkhana, Shivajinagar, Camp and Swargate were suburbs. Unlike in the Camp area, there were no outsiders, so there was no need for hotels, except for a few lodges where travellers in transit could spend a night or two. The only restaurants were small tea shops or sweet shops with huge kadhais for frying batata vadas and kanda bhajias.

Poona people were mild-tempered and kind, and never held resentment or grudges against any person or community. They were less demanding and nowhere near as aggressive as some of the people from North. However, I did find that if you were not a local it was hard to gain acceptance. I had picked up the language and could easily pass as a local. But those who knew that I had come from Karachi would always consider me a foreigner. In today's rapidly shrinking world with a high migrant working population and elastic boundaries, this syndrome might seem odd but it is one which has afflicted the locals of small communities everywhere in the world.

Now more than ever my mind was restless, looking for options. Though I was learning a little, my work was tedious and repetitive. Even when customers came, no effort was required to sell. There would be some minimal negotiations, and loans issued or money returned. I remember in particular one collection case I had, was recovering money from a goldsmith who had his shop near the Mandai, the main vegetable market of Poona. He was a regular defaulter, and once he had passed his date of payment, I would sometimes have to sit at his shop for days on end, simply waiting for a customer to enter. Once he made a sale and received money, it would not be possible for him to continue pleading lack of funds and he would hand over some amount from what he had received from the customer.

All day long, from morning to night, my life was a deadening routine. I knew I had to get out and do something more meaningful and make a better future for myself.

Sometime in early 1947, my aunt and uncle left Poona to visit Shikarpur to find a match for their second and third daughters, the eldest being already married. Lachhmandas, my cousin who was one year older than me, was left in charge of the business. My duty was to see to him and the younger ones, taking care of their requirements both at home and at the pedhi. We followed our routine as usual, but there were two incidents which I will always remember.

One morning, I was sent to the Bank of India near the City Post Office with a bearer cheque to withdraw Rs. 500, with instructions to ask for ten-rupee notes, which we could use for lending as well as at home. By now I knew the procedure well. I had to collect a token, give it to the cashier, and wait for my token number to be announced.

When I received the money I counted it and found that I had been given sixty notes. A little puzzled, I counted again. The cashier was watching and asked me what the matter was. By now I was able to communicate in Marathi well and requested another look at the cheque. He handed it over, and I confirmed that it was indeed a cheque for Rs. 500. I now returned the bundle of notes for him to count again.

He noticed his mistake at once with shock. He had given me an additional amount exceeding his salary for the entire month! If I had not returned it, he would have been liable to pay that Rs. 100 to the bank from his own means. In those days, the bank had a procedure of counting cash at the end of the day, with any shortfall to be compensated by the cashier.

In gratitude, he came out from behind the barrier and literally bowed his thanks to me. I was a little embarrassed and didn't feel that I had done anything special. I never spoke about this incident at home, but it was a source of happiness to me that I was now always welcomed with respect at the bank and the cashier in particular treated me with great deference.

On another occasion, I was walking towards our home when I saw the entire building begin to collapse in front of my eyes. There were loud, alarming sounds of creaking and crashing, and people screaming in fright and calling out to each other in panic. Fortunately, the children were away at school. As it crumbled and fell, people fled from the building. Luckily everyone inside managed to escape before it disintegrated completely. Watching from across the street, the thought came to me that I should run for help. I did not know anyone in Poona except for a few business acquaintances of my uncle, and I raced to the shop of one whose son was a friend of Lachhman, thinking that I could call the boy to help me. However, when his father heard my gasped-out story, he shooed me away. "Go to the police!" he said, "Go to the municipality! Why are you bothering us?"

A little bemused, I returned to the site where our home had been, only to find a crowd of people looking for me under the debris, and I received another shouting for running away. It seemed they thought I had purposely run away to trouble them. I was quite used to this type of treatment, but that didn't make it any less unpleasant.

That night we were given shelter by one of my uncle's business acquaintances. Next day Lachhman and I found a small and rather dirty hovel into which we moved, along with the few belongings we had been able to retrieve. Lachhman had sent a telegram to his parents and they returned from Shikarpur with his sisters. We continued to live in the new place with a similar life as before, until sometime towards the end of 1947 when my uncle told me that he had received a letter from my eldest brother in Karachi saying that they were thinking of coming to Poona.

There was no thought in my mind but sheer delight. I waited eagerly for more news. I had not been particularly pining away for my family, but once I knew their arrival was imminent, I began to long for the comfort of having my own people around me.

Today I understand the trauma that my family and thousands like them went through. The sudden upheaval and violence around them had been terrifying and confusing. All of a sudden, they had been pushed out of their home, forced to make arrangements to cross the border and somehow settle in a strange land.

Having been mobile from a very young age, I was naturally not very sensitive to their plight at the time. Today I understand the magnitude of being snatched out of your homeland, leaving the place of your ancestors, losing forever the sense of connection to your own land, and having to start all over again. Worst of all was to know that you would never be able to go home because your home no longer existed.

However, in 1947, for me to have my family, my mother, brothers and sisters, come to Poona to be with me was cause for rejoicing rather than despair. It never struck me that they were coming here with heavy hearts, and that they had chosen Poona of all the possible places they could have settled in only because I was here. It never struck me that for them to leave Karachi was a matter of deepest mourning.

For centuries the Sindhi Hindus and Muslims had lived side-by-side like brothers. We went to our temple and they went to their mosque – that was the only difference. Both communities were deeply influenced by the Sufi creed of respect and reverence for others and equal treatment for all; love for all creatures, polite speech, and most importantly, tolerance for other faiths. Sufism observes that we come into this world empty handed and leave it empty handed. All we really own in this life are our actions. It was this deeply-ingrained philosophy that gave my community the strength to single-mindedly leave everything behind and move on, and then single-mindedly build it all back again, and more.

At the time when partition struck us, it simply did not register that we no longer lived in India but in a new country, Pakistan. My mother, grandmother, brothers and sisters and thousands of others like them, continued to live at home, and tried to live the lives they had always led, believing that, like the Muslims in India, we too could remain in peace in our native land.

Our beautiful, important city had been chosen as the new nation's capital. Hordes of Muslims from East Punjab and U.P. who preferred to settle in the newly created Muslim state of Pakistan now started flowing into Karachi. Ruthless and demanding, they considered it their right to walk into any Hindu house or establishment and take it over. Incidents of lawlessness began to rise. It became dangerous for girls to go out in the streets alone. Watching with horror and despair, the Hindus began to understand that things could never go back to being what they used to. They packed a few suitcases, left their property and memories behind forever.

In his letters to my uncle, my brother wrote about this violence, and their fear. These days the expression "Sindhi diaspora" is a familiar one, and indicates a people who have lost their roots. For us, it was the reality we lived. Many of the rural Sindhis uprooted themselves and moved to Jaipur, Ajmer, Ahmedabad, or towns and villages near the border. A large majority of middle-class and upper middle-class Sindhis with some money or connections, such as my family, bought their passage on the Scindia liner which had begun operating two or three times a week from Karachi to Bombay to service this new flood of traffic. Many arrived in Bombay and were transported directly to refugee camps in Kalyan,

Ulhasnagar, Pimpri and other nearby places where they lived for a few weeks or months while the men of the family travelled over the country looking for places to settle and some type of viable sustenance. A very large number of us carried out a similar exercise in other countries and set up little shops or businesses in every corner of the globe from Hong Kong to Tenerife to Nigeria. Still others, some of the wealthy landlords, chose to stay on in the land that had been cultivated by their families for generations, unwilling to forsake the comfort and security of home and risk poverty and deprivation in strange, faraway lands. A few of them converted to Islam, or at least changed their names if not their beliefs. A large majority of these unfortunate souls were threatened and forced to leave. Many of them were killed.

Our entire community watched in confusion and torment as others took over and ravaged our homes, assets and all our possessions, driving us out with nothing.

It was the biggest displacement in history. In the struggle to relocate and survive, the Sindhi community as a whole focused all its effort and energy into adapting to new environments and claiming them as home. Economic survival was the key challenge.

As a community, we tend to be creative, enterprising and proud group. Putting aside our rage and grief at this terrible thing that had happened to us, most of us established ourselves in various locations around the globe, and soon began to flourish. Though primarily successful in business, today you will find Sindhis at the top of every field including medicine, literature, philanthropy, or the armed services. No Sindhi, no matter how poor, would ever stoop to begging. During partition you could see young Sindhi boys selling trinkets on the local trains in Bombay. Not only were these children homeless but many had been orphaned by partition. Struck as they were by trauma and poverty, they would take money only in exchange for goods. I too had once been suddenly deprived of a carefree life of comfort. I could well identify with how they felt.

The intense striving to adapt and prosper had the expensive and rather tragic outcome of losing us our language and, as a result, our culture. Many families of my generation spoke to their children only in the local language of the place they moved to. They never spoke about their past, deliberately casting aside the memories of their native towns, familiar sights and sounds, or incidents from their childhood. Choosing instead to immerse themselves in local and often materialistic matters, they severed the oral tradition that links a people to their past.

As I write this, a few weeks before my 78th birthday, I continue to long for my ancestral home in Shikarpur. The nostalgia of my own home town, friends whose families had been friends with my family for generation, with whom we celebrated our religious functions is very strong. Though Punjab too was partitioned causing tremendous bloodshed and suffering, atleast some part of it was retained and the Indian Punjabis do have a land they can call their own. But for us Sindhis, nothing remains – nothing at all. We are scattered across the globe.

My children's generation were cut off even further from their moorings. There was just no home town to return to, no matter how infrequently, which could have provided a reference or even a reminder of the age-old traditions, stories grandmothers told, or lullabies that mothers sang. There were no books for them to read. Even those who were lucky enough to pick up some words of their mother tongue would never learn our beautiful script. Our language is on the verge of becoming extinct, and along with it all the extensive Sindhi poetry and philosophy is lost almost beyond recall.

When my family finally fled Karachi, they travelled by camel cart to the port, dressed like Muslims.

By this time, looting and killings were being reported, curfew and other restrictions were being imposed, and stories of the mass slaughter on the trains had stirred us all with terror.

Bhagwandas was now married. His wife Sulochana was expecting their first child and she had been sent ahead to safety in Bombay with her mother. My family decided that they would travel by ship. Along with a few personal belongings, they also carried some open bags containing fruits and vegetables. These were not just their sustenance for the journey, but also a secret hiding place for their valuables. They sliced off the tops of melons, scooped out the seeds, hid my mother's few remaining pieces of personal jewellery inside, and then replaced the tops.

They arrived in Bombay and were given a little space in a small room in Girgaum where they slept on the floor. Surely the leaders of our country who had got us our Independence had known that this was going to happen to us! But now there was nothing anyone could do.

My family had decided to move to Poona. Bombay, they had felt, was not a city for children to grow up in. There was no place for them to play and learn. I was already settled in Poona, and though I may have been only 17, I would be able to help them bridge the gaps of language, food and customs.

Completely oblivious to their dilemma, the only thought in my mind at this time was that I would finally be able to live in my own home with my own family. At last I would be able to start some type of business of my own, and look after myself. I looked forward to their arrival with great excitement, quite unaware of the national fervour about Independence, and vaguely wondering why crowds of people were marching about and cheering, letting off firecrackers and playing loud music when it was neither Diwali nor Id or even the festival of Ganesh Chaturthi.

All the exploration I had done around the city now stood me in good stead. By the end of 1947, in anticipation of my family's arrival, I had located a small flat of two and a half bedrooms in a wada in the centre of the city. My uncle paid three months rent in advance, dipping into my wages accumulated over the last year and a half.

Ramchand, my elder brother, was still working with Mulchand Chandrabhan & Co. in Bombay. Two of my sisters were already married. The rest of the family, my three brothers, three sisters, my mother and grandmother, arrived in Poona. My uncle considered it unnecessary for me to go to the station to receive them and brought them in a tonga to Sugandhi Wada, 485 Narayan Peth, which was to be our address for many years to come. My uncle and aunt set up our home with the few provisions and utensils necessary to start our new life.

All of us had been issued landing certificates. One had been collected on my behalf as well. These served not only as a proof of identity but also for the purpose of claiming property or some compensation. By and large the amounts allotted were insignificant compared to what had

39

been lost. Till today I have never met a single Sindhi who availed this government offering though am sure many did, In fact, such were our levels of distress that through sheer inertia, many of us lost opportunities to purchase land offered by the government at low rates.

Narayan Peth is a locality adjoining Lakshmi Road, the central and most important road of the Poona city area. To establish a Sindhi family in this Brahmin stronghold near Lokhande Talim was unusual at the time, and was possible only because Sakhrani's firm had been established here for decades. Most of the Sindhi and Punjabi refugees who arrived in Poona settled around the Camp area which was more cosmopolitan, or in the leftover spaces between the Maharashtrian and non-Marathi-speaking areas, bordering the eastern peths, Bhavanipeth and Nanapeth, which acted as a dividing line between the locals and non-locals, and the market at the end of the Cantonment. The government set up a camp for the refugees near Pimpri, while others settled around the railway station.

For us it was a big advantage living in the city and absorbing the local language and ways, and becoming thoroughly integrated into the society of our adopted home. However, this also meant that the women of the family were isolated from the warmth of the rich community life that they had been used to in Karachi. My grandmother pined for her large and comfortable home in Shikarpur. She missed the other family members who had lived in the haveli, and all the other friends and relatives who had been such an important part of her daily life. Here we slept crowded together, and besides all the other compromises in comfort and standard of living, we had to use a community toilet downstairs, an indignity to which she never adjusted. My mother on the other hand never grumbled though she too held her memories dear. Since my father's death she had been silent and reconciled to her fate.

After a few days, my uncle handed over my remaining dues to my mother. This, and the Rs. 30 monthly salary he would continue to pay me, was all we had. We had to seek other opportunities, and were confident that they would come our way.

My younger brothers and sisters were suffering their own trials. In Maharashtra in those days, people were more accustomed to eating rotis made of other grains such as makkai, jawar and bajra rather than wheat flour. My siblings found the food strange and unpalatable and longed for the chapattis we were used to. They fell ill with stomach ailments and heat boils.

There was no Sindhi school to admit them to, and the local schools were not willing to accept them without school-leaving certificates. We turned to the Gujarati school which was run by a charitable trust and expected no fees to be paid. Over the next few years all of them completed their school education in Gujarati, making progress with difficulty because of the language barrier.

As for me, I was now bursting with excitement at the idea that at long last I could start some kind of business of my own. When I rode around town doing errands for my family or for my uncle's firm, I would glance up at the sky and inquire, "What should I do? What am I going to do?"

One day soon after my family arrived in Poona, the city erupted in violence. From our window we could see mobs and fires raging. It was the historic day, the 30th of January 1948, when Mahatma Gandhi had been killed. The assassin was from Poona and there were riots with homes and shops being ravaged and destroyed. I saw people breaking into buildings, shouting and looting. Along with the anger and outrage that swept the city, there seemed also to be an opinion that the Father of the Nation had given away too much and had compromised us Sindhis. Over a period, the violence died down, leaving only bitter feelings which took much longer to subside.

Before this incident, I did not know much about Gandhi except that he was one of the few very important people that everyone spoke about. In the years to come I learnt more about him from newspapers, books and movies.

In today's world, youngsters are exposed to so much information and different types of interaction that it gives them knowledge and sophistication at an early age. It is difficult to explain how different things were in my time. My awareness of the world around me grew slowly.

It was not possible for me to look for another better-paying job as that would have been an insult to my uncle. We had no capital and would not be able to start our own business. Casting about for options, one day I received an unexpected letter from my friend Thakur, with whom I had been corresponding infrequently, informing me that the Nagdev family had moved to Bombay after partition. I went at once to meet him. Thakur was delighted to see me, and invited me to stay with him in Bombay for as long as I liked. This was extremely generous of him, since space was at a premium in Bombay then just as it is today, and not many people would consider extending such hospitality. But that was not all. Thakur's family were in the wholesale cloth business, and he now gave me a large lot of cloth left over from one of his firm's consignments. He urged me to carry it back with me to Poona, insisting that I pay for it only after I had sold the entire quantity. I had been shy of keeping in touch with Thakur ever since the social gap came between us, but now the feeling of having someone who cared about me and who trusted me filled me with happiness.

I rushed back home with the bundles of cloth, excited that we were finally in business!

My uncle Harbhagwandas greeted my decision with great dismay and tried to persuade me to change my mind. He kindly suggested that though he had no objection to my staying with my family, I should continue working with him. I declined quite politely.

We now had to find a way to sell our precious stock. We had no shop or any type of outlet, so Bhagwandas and I decided to try standing on the road and selling to passers-by.

On the first day we set up our new trade on Lakshmi Road next to Variety Stores. We held some bundles of cloth in our arms and called out to passers-by, offering them the best quality at the best prices. However, buying things off the street was an entirely unknown practice and the people we hailed gave us uncertain looks and hurried past without stopping. Perhaps it was us refugees who introduced this type of innovation into Indian retailing. Unfortunately, my brother and I were ahead of our time and had very little success. We spent a few months selling the stock given to us by Thakur in this manner, but it was time-consuming and did not yield sufficient returns for us to run the house.

My former employers were calling me back, offering to raise my salary. But I had tasted freedom, and though my income was now uncertain, I had no intention of returning. Various commercial opportunities came to us through Bhajandas Ahuja, Daya's husband. They had settled in Bombay after closing the dealership in Amritsar, and were looking after the family money-lending business. For a brief period we tried dealing in plastic soap boxes, Meccano sets, and various other imported items.

I had already observed the lifestyle, approach, and opportunities of the Poona shopkeepers and was doubtful whether there was much scope for me in this area. Now a new opportunity arose through Ahujasaab. One of their clients, a Parsi gentleman, had borrowed money to set up an outfit manufacturing electrical accessories. He had been unable to keep to his repayment schedule and some of his stock was repossessed. My brother-in-law now offered this stock to my brothers and me to start a new business for ourselves. Eagerly, we transported the material, ceiling roses, switches, and other electrical goods, to Poona.

Over the past few months, I had been to every corner of Poona for my collection duties. My elder brothers, however, knew neither the local language nor anything about the city. I realised with pride that it was all up to me. I filled my samples into a large canvas bag and walked around, looking for shops that would be interested in buying these items. For several days, I set off early morning in search and returned home late at night, exhausted but unsuccessful. There was no specific electrical market as most cities have today, and the shops were scattered in different areas and streets. To look carefully for shops in every locality on foot was pointlessly tiring. We decided to rent a bicycle so that I could ride around with two of the bags filled with samples slung on its handles.

I would wake early morning and set off, scouring the streets one by one, entering each shop that seemed it might be interested in electrical accessories. By now I knew the pattern of shop timings in Poona quite well, but being enthusiastic and inexperienced I would often arrive too early and have to wait outside until it opened. I would then go in and introduce myself. However, I was just a young boy without a company to back me, and no type of track record or history or relationship I could quote. The shopkeepers I approached were not overly busy, but they would often ignore me or, worse, shoo me away. I was just a nuisance getting in their way. I would wait patiently, requesting that they give me just a few minutes to see what I had brought. Some of them, before listening to me or even looking at what I had in the bag, would laugh at me for coming to them so early in the morning. "I haven't sold anything, I haven't even seen a single customer's face, and you expect me to buy!" they would scoff. So I would sit quietly and wait, or sometimes stand outside and wait, holding my cycle for an hour or two until they had made a few sales, and then open my bag and show a few samples. After that they would say, "Why should I buy from you! I can go and buy the same thing from Bombay myself at a much lower price!"

One of the big problems I faced was that in the late 1940s, goods produced by small Indian manufacturers were considered unreliable and of poor quality – which in fact they often were. People only respected the well-known British brands. This was one of the reasons that the Parsi gentleman was struggling. However, I never thought about this. My only concern was that I had to sell, and would set out each morning determined to find buyers. I would visit each shop, waiting until I got the attention of the decision-maker. I would politely display my wares one at a time, describing all the features and benefits in detail. I would answer every query sincerely. If they said there was no requirement at the moment, I would thank them and say I would come back in a few days.

I had worked in sales situations for long enough to know how to make a customer feel important. If someone got particularly annoyed at my persistence and ordered me to leave, I would do so, and simply wait for a few days before going back and quietly trying again. I never allowed the feeling of rejection to influence my next action, but kept calmly focussed on my objective instead. For every success, I would allow myself a few silent moments of celebration, and would immediately put my mind and efforts back into making the next sale. Every day I was looking for more shops, more sources to whom I could supply.

I never took "NO" for an answer, but would always try again.

Sometimes; they showed interest in some of the products, but would be unwilling to trust a new brand. Since I had not paid anything for this stock, I could afford to hand over a few samples without payment, in anticipation of sale. However this now meant that collection became a separate activity. I had to keep a record of all my transactions, and began noting down the shops I had sold to, the address and telephone number, name of the person in authority, which item they had accepted, and how many pieces. I could still barely write, but it gave me a special type of pleasure to organize myself by maintaining this record.

After a few weeks I would have to come back and face the double challenge of collecting the money I was owed as well as making a further sale. Once again, I would often be ignored or turned away. There were many occasions on which I would be given part payment and asked to come back later for the rest.

I soon learnt that I should reserve the evening for this activity, as there was a chance that by this time they would have made some collection from which my payment could be made. The best time would be around 9 o'clock at night, just before the shop closed for the day.

The Poona shops would close for lunch and a siesta, a habit that persists even today in some quarters. This did not suit my working style at all, but I had no choice but to head home myself during this interval, annoyed and frustrated at the idea that anyone could sleep for three hours in the middle of the day. In many areas of the world, it is customary to take a break from work to cope with the heat of the day – but that was no excuse in Poona where the temperature was pleasant right through the year!

I had to make many visits for each transaction, but over a period, my record of sales, collections, and further sales began to grow slowly. So it happened that my stock gradually reduced and I went eagerly back to Bombay where the Parsi gentleman was more than willing to part with some more material without any payment in advance, since I had proved myself capable of selling it.

Within a few months, the shopkeepers had started recognizing me. They now began to place small orders, giving me samples themselves and asking me to bring back a few pieces of certain items for them from Lohar Chawl, the electrical accessories market in Bombay, which they knew I visited regularly. This saved them the bother and expense of travelling to Bombay, or of buying from other Poona wholesalers whose margins would have been much higher. Delighted to oblige, I began to increase my range of products. Even with a good mark-up as commission for my time and effort, they would still benefit on price. As for me, I now found that I was earning as much as ten or even twenty rupees every day, the amount that I had previously got after working an entire month! By the end of the month, I had earned a few hundred rupees. This was more like it!

The new-found prosperity never tempted us to spend money on ourselves or to increase the family's standard of living in any way. In fact, it never occurred to us to do this. The years of hardship, and the sudden displacement, had made us focussed only on settling ourselves and setting up a source of livelihood that would never fail us. Surplus money, if any, had to be immediately reinvested into the business to bring us greater productivity, profit and stability. I began to learn about the different types of electrical products in popular use. Some of the brands had complicated names that I could not pronounce but I soon became familiar with them. As I supplied to the shops, I also studied the other products and equipment they stocked.

Very soon, I had a good grasp of the various companies and all the competing products, with a thorough knowledge of the price, features, and limitations or special properties of each. From switches and ceiling roses we went on to different types of electrical wires and cables, and I now also began to bring samples of items like irons, table lamps, immersion heaters and hotplates, and take orders for them. Adding products in this manner, our business grew steadily.

As I worked continuously to improve my product knowledge, I also took care to think about what my customers wanted, and what would bring them the best benefit. Some were looking for quality and durability, others were looking for price, yet others had requirements for specific features or were working within a specific market. I could tell each one of my buyers which of these products was exactly right for his particular needs, why he should switch from one to the other, and offer him supplementary products which would enhance his current range. Most important of all, I found that my habit of buying carefully, testing each lot for defects and discarding rejects, made it possible for me to assure my customers got only high-quality goods. I remembered how my grandmother had always taken me to the same sweet shop in Shikarpur because that was the place with sweets of the best quality ingredients and taste. Sure enough, my customers began to trust me and I began to get regular repeat orders.

Within a year of starting, our business had grown and we needed more resources. Ramchand quit his job but stayed on in Bombay to arrange our supplies, and by 1954 we rented a small shop in Lohar Chawl to store material. I would write down our requirements, and though my scribbled instructions were part Sindhi and part English, Ramchand was somehow able to decipher them.

My trips to Bombay now reduced, but I continued to travel occasionally. I would have to leave home early in the morning and my grandmother now became my alarm clock. The milk was delivered at 5 a.m. and she would bring it in and wake me with a cup of tea. I would get ready and leave. By this time my mother would be up, and she would sit cross-legged in meditation for an hour before gently rousing the others with a cup of milk or tea.

I would park my cycle at the railway station, taking the Poona Mail train to Bombay, and returning home by the late night passenger train. This was called the milkman's train, because it brought the early-morning milk deliveries into the city. It was a slow passenger train, and from Dehu Road station onwards the milkmen would climb aboard, heaving and clanking their large brass buckets of buffalo milk on board.

A ticket to Bombay cost the considerable sum of Rs. 3.50, and I often travelled without buying one. At that time, the need to economise was foremost in my mind and it did not occur to me that I was doing anything wrong. I did feel a little nervous about getting caught and deliberately travelled on the slow and crowded trains which were not of particular interest to the ticket collectors.

There was one occasion on which I had a narrow escape. Stepping sleepily out of the milkman's train early one morning, I walked along with a thick crowd towards the gate of the Poona station. The ticket inspector was randomly stopping passengers and checking their tickets. As usual, I was looking downward so that he would not catch my eye and question me. However, this time before I could sidle out and escape, I was stopped. When I did not respond, he gestured to me to wait while he attended to the other passengers streaming out of the station. My heart beating fast, I stood next to him, my hands behind my back. I was very tired, having had only a disturbed sleep on the journey, I leaned back against the railing. Suddenly, I felt a ticket thrust into my hand! Without turning around, I knew that one of the passengers who had crossed the barrier had somehow taken it into his head to save me from my plight and slipped his ticket across to me. Finally the crowd thinned, and the ticket inspector turned to confront me. I quietly held out the ticket in my hand. He looked at it, puzzled, and asked me why I had been waiting if I had had a ticket all the while! I shrugged my shoulders and told him that he had asked me to wait, so I had waited. I hurried off, looking around for the angel who had come to my rescue, but there were only stray passers-by going about their business and no one paid any particular attention to me. He had obviously not waited to hear my thanks.

Later in life also I had many experiences when I was in trouble and help came to me suddenly, and from totally unexpected sources. I would think back to this moment when I was a youngster, struggling to make something of myself, and smile. It was a good feeling to know that there was some unseen power looking after me.

During this period I began to learn a few words of English, and slowly started becoming familiar with the script.

Our business began to grow. The volume of goods to be brought to Poona was now so large that Ramchand would have to hire a handcart to carry them to his shop. He would pack the material into boxes, and then send the consignment to our shop in a lorry.

The lorry would arrive at our building in Narayan Peth. We would unload it and bring all the goods upstairs to our house. We brothers worked together, unpacking and sorting it out, and I would begin the process of distribution, filling the goods as usual into canvas bags and transporting them by bicycle. Feeling a little secure that our business was growing, we now bought some furniture for the house.

We also rented a small space under the staircase of a building opposite the Jogeshwari Temple in a congested area of the city where we could unload our stock instead of carrying it up the stairs to our home. There was a wooden partition which we could lock when we went home at night.

Very soon we also installed a telephone under the staircase so that customers could phone us with inquiries or orders. We put in a parallel line at our home, and this was such a novelty that neighbours would often stop by to marvel in admiration.

We registered our new business as a partnership firm of Ramchand Bhagwandas & Co., which is what our father's firm in Karachi had been called. We printed letterheads for our communication and documentation.

My younger brother Kishanchand was still studying but he would sometimes come and sit at the shop with Bhagwandas, attending customers or answering the phone. It took some months before our company was able to employ any staff, and until then Kishan and I continued to do all the cleaning, carrying boxes of material up the stairs and other menial tasks.

By now I could write well enough to record my phone orders. We had begun doing very well in this regard. Many of the electrical shops in Poona were run by elderly people. They were only too happy to have someone bring them goods from Bombay. This brought big advantages for both sides. For me the profit on selling something that the dealers had asked for was much more than trying to sell my own range of products which may or may not be useful to them. For them the benefit was that I was not only bringing goods of the best quality, but also giving them a good price. In addition, they were particularly pleased with the credit facility I readily extended.

All my years in collection had taught me about how to identify parties who were creditworthy. I knew that one could never tell a person's financial standing or reliability from appearances. Many who appeared to be well-off were actually living on someone else's money. Someone with a large and impressive shop could well be fronting a failing business. While I sat and waited, I overheard the conversation the shopkeeper had with his employees and customers, and observed the frequency and quantity of sale. From this I became aware, quite unconsciously, of the level of his business. I also learnt a lot about competitors, customer requirements, the reputation of other shopkeepers, and other key market information. It was a small community, and I soon understood it extremely well.

By and large, my initiative of extending credit turned out to be a smart business practice. We were now also able to get credit from my suppliers at Lohar Chawl. One thing we were very particular about was to always make payments on time. The biggest learning of all my work experience so far was that in business, your reputation is your most valuable asset. There is only one way to build one's creditworthiness – to demonstrate again and again that you are indeed creditworthy by making sure you always pay on time. We did. Our suppliers, delighted with our growing business, continued to give us every kind of support.

This period of growing maturity brought other revelations as well. It was at this time that I first began to understand what my brothers had done by giving away all the family property and assets. It was an inbuilt tradition of family principle and such severe integrity that they had upheld and honoured all the debts despite knowing of the awful consequences to the many people who depended on them after our father's death. Our home and garden, our carriage and servants, even the family heirlooms meant nothing compared to our honour. We would never regret the fact that we would all, including the children of the family, now have to struggle together to meet our most basic needs. The alternative, that of losing our good name, was infinitely worse. We understood that money will come and go, depending on the market and customer demands; the only tangibles actually within one's control were one's own actions.

The truth is that instead of doing what they had done, if my brothers had decided to retain our family wealth we would have lost it all anyway when partition took place. We would have arrived in our new home with nothing, not even our reputation. The taint of shame would always have hung over our family.

I also learnt at this time that my dear grandmother was actually my father's stepmother. This naturally did not affect our relationship at all, and we continued to be extremely fond of each other. She had two daughters of her own, one whom I had stayed with when I first came to Poona, and another who had died young in Karachi. All this made no difference at all to her feelings for me, or mine for her. Ever since I was very young, we had always had a special bond. It was she who would get up early to see that I had something to eat before I left for Bombay, or when I came home late. This is one of the reasons that I have little regard for stereotypes and prefer to make my own assessment of people and situations rather than blindly succumbing to labels.

Bhagwandas and his wife Sulochana were in Poona. Ramchand was also married now, and he and his wife Leela were still living in Bombay. Over the next few years, two of my younger sisters also got married. Laxmi, closest in age to me, married Kishandas Bathija, who was in the money-lending business, the sister younger to her, Indra, married Manumal Bajaj, whose family was in the cloth business. Both lived in Bombay. My mother, sister-in-law, and grandmother managed the house. Kishan had finished his schooling and came to join the business so now there were four of us brothers working together, with Ramchand in Bombay, and Bhagwandas, Kishan and me in Poona.

Our business of supplying electrical accessories to Poona retailers continued to grow in this manner. While I once rode around the city making my deliveries on a rented bicycle, we now bought a bicycle for ourselves. However, since three of us brothers were sharing it, this still meant that I would sometimes have to do my rounds on foot!

In early 1951, we rented another apartment on the second floor of the same building which held our stores under the staircase, 675 Budhwar Peth, which we converted into a retail shop. Our customers had got used to our speedy delivery and good quality products, and thought nothing of climbing the two flights of stairs to the shop. Our reputation spread, and we now began to attract retail customers such as electrical wiremen. Initially, the shopkeepers to whom we had been supplying were annoyed with us for selling directly to their customers, but they accepted that we were giving them products of the best quality, excellent margins, and prompt delivery.

For us, there were multiple advantages in having a place to stock our goods. We could buy in bulk and supply at the most competitive rates, and would always have stocks of what our customers ordered. Our deliveries would be prompt, almost instant, and our range of stock made us a one-stop shop for our customers. As our business grew, so did our credibility, and soon there were traders coming from as far as Kolhapur and Solapur to us for their purchases.

As per the name of the shop, Ramchand Bhagwandas & Co., the business was owned by my brothers, and Kishan and I being the younger ones, knew that this was as it should be. We did not mind at all. Kishan soon became as conversant with the streets of the city and as fluent in the local language as I was. However, I continued to be responsible for most of the operational activities such as supplying and collecting, and most of the planning and implementation was also mine. For a long time, every ground-level business decision pertaining to product or customer was taken only by me.

In addition to buying and selling electrical accessories, we had also begun to provide some small electrical services ourselves. Right from the beginning, Kishan had a very high technical aptitude. As he sat in the shop with Bhagwandas, attending customers and writing accounts, he began to take the electrical appliances apart to repair them. He would never make the mistake of opening something up, making minor readjustment or replacement required and returning it, as good as new, to his customer. Instead he had learnt to tell them that it might take some time and he would give them the estimate in two or three days, thus ensuring the price he deserved for his efforts. Ingenious in every way, he soon began to participate in electrical jobs, such as laying cables, through other contractors at the sites of new buildings. At one point he manufactured his own line of irons. He picked up a flat casting, got it turned at a fabricator's unit, put an electrical element inside, covered the bottom with an asbestos sheet, and began marketing his own brand of dhobi istri, showing his customers how their clothes now no longer needed to be victims of coal burns from the dhobi's heavy-duty iron. The only Indian manufacturer of electrical irons at that time was BEST, the Bombay Electrical Supply and Transport Co. People used to improvise their own irons by filling brass or copper utensils with coal and running them over their formal wear, or risk the little coal holes dhobis invariably returned clothes with. To service this new line, we began to rent a new shop at 484 Budhwar Peth.

Sometime in 1952, tube lights began to become popular. I remember installing tube lights at a church near Rasta Peth. Two nuns came to our shop and I set up the light for them that would shine all night behind a statue of Jesus Christ.

Our company was doing well, but at around this time I began to realise that we had reached the ceiling of this type of business. I was not party to any of the financial decisions and had no idea on what basis those decisions were made. I never concerned myself with things which were outside my control and responsibility, and was completely preoccupied with my daily activities. Foremost in my mind were collecting orders, making prompt deliveries, collecting payments, and getting fresh orders. I could see that the scale of our earnings had gone up from tens to hundreds and now to thousands. The stock value was in tens of thousands. However, though I understood that we were doing well, my instinct told me that there was a limit to expansion in this business, and that mere trading, and earning small in-between profits, would never give me the kind of future I knew I must build for myself.

At the end of each day when we met at home, I would try to convince my elder brothers that we needed to branch out and start some kind of new operations. There were five of us, and I could see very clearly that two small shops were not going to provide any kind of sustenance and future for the five families that we would soon have. However they were wary of my ideas. I found it difficult to share my views and plans with them. I often found myself get into heated argument with them, which I invariably lost. This made me feel undervalued. Though I was the one with the most experience of the market, they still considered me to be a child. I felt stifled and frustrated.

As my ambitions grew, the lack of acknowledgement and support from my brothers became too oppressive for me to bear and finally, in extreme frustration, I decided that I must leave home.

There was a gentleman I knew who had worked with me at Wadhuram Chhabria, the building contractor in Karachi who had employed me to keep an eye on the Pathan truck drivers. After partition, he had written to me that he and his family had moved to Jaipur. Since we had maintained occasional correspondence, he had been sympathetic to my plight and had shown kindness.

Without telling anyone, I packed my bags and set off to his address in Jaipur with one thousand rupees in my pocket.

After hearing my story, my friend soothed and encouraged me and then made me sit down and write a letter to my mother explaining why I had left, assuring her that I was well, and that I would soon come back home. I was comfortable at my friend's place and began helping him in his work and thinking about business opportunities for myself, but when my brother wrote back requesting him to send me home immediately, I had no choice but to return. I felt perturbed and powerless, and very disappointed. However, soon after this incident, I took permission from the elders in the family and went to live in Bangalore where my mother's sister had settled with her family. Her husband Dhanrajmull Chawla was keen to start an electrical shop like the one we had in Poona. On the basis of my three or four years of experience in running such an establishment, he rented a place and we set up store. The idea was to continue receiving material from Bombay, which I would distribute as I had done in Poona, and he would manage inventory, accounts, walk-in customers and so on. Very soon, however, we ran into supply problems. Travel to Bombay took 48 hours, making it too far away for me to make quick trips to bring the supplies myself. After several months, we decided to close shop, and I returned to Poona. Soon after that Chawlasaab and his family also joined us in Poona and subsequently joined our business.

I returned home and soon got back to work. Business was good and I threw myself into my daily work with the same involvement and passion as before. As before, convinced that there was neither growth nor progress in our present operations, I continued to look for new opportunities to expand the scope and scale of the business. It was a source of strength and comfort to me that though my elder brothers were hesitant and conservative, my younger brother Kishan believed in me completely and put all his energy into contributing towards my efforts. He shared the same enthusiasm, confidence and excitement in continuously building and growing our business together.

At this time, I used to get a little pocket money to take care of my personal expenses. My mother was also given a fixed amount for our household expenses, and invariably struggled to make ends meet. It never even occurred to any of us that we could have easily bought a home for ourselves. We continued to rent 485 Narayan Peth, and I was completely committed to this life of waking early, working all day, and coming home late at night to eat and sleep, only to set off again early next day, because I knew this was the only way to succeed. I never thought of it as discomfort or struggle. It never occurred to me that my life was difficult. On the rare occasions that I now looked up at the sky, it was because I knew that was where I wanted to reach.

3

Karve Road, Poona, 1952

MEN AND MACHINES

"For growth, one must continuously innovate. One must constantly observe customer requirements, changing habits, and market trends. One must remain always at the forefront of discovery, understanding emerging technologies and always looking for lucrative ways in which to put them to use. I had learnt these principles through my observation and experience, and they have always remained at the core of my working methods."

Poona had been selected as the headquarters of the Southern Area Command of the Indian Army by the British in the early nineteenth century. Being well connected and conveniently close to Bombay, a major port, Pune was well protected, as it was sufficiently inland and surrounded by a range of hills. There was flat land too, where, as it turned out later, an airstrip could be constructed. The climate and people were both congenial.

The Indian Army had been trained and developed by Britain for its own purposes, to defend the territory of India from invasion as well as a warlike force to deploy in other lands. More than one and a quarter million Indian soldiers volunteered to fight for Britain in World War I a figure larger in number than all the Scots, Welsh and Irish combined. More than two and a quarter million Indian soldiers fought alongside Allied troops in World War II. Indian troops served not only in Europe, but in all the other major theatres of war.

The British had followed a strategy of recruiting Indian soldiers primarily from martial races such as the Marathas, Sikhs, Rajputs, Coorgs and

57

Pimpri, 2008: K. P. and P. P. Chhabria with their
first braiding machine.

Gurkhas, who saw fighting as a noble profession that would bring honour to themselves and their villages. In the matter of weaponry too, the British followed the strategy of not only importing their finest war machinery to India, but also setting up several ordnance factories all over the country to produce a range of equipment, arms and ammunition.

Through taxation, India raised two major war donations for Britain, each amounting to millions of pounds. Besides money and warriors, India provided many of the vital supplies for the war; jute for sandbags, cotton cloth for uniforms, vast quantities of tea, wheat and rice which fed not only the army but British civilians also. The British had created forces in India that they once described as "a barracks in the Oriental seas from which we may draw any number of troops without paying for them".

By the end of World War II, this barracks was sadly depleted of both people and equipment. Many stations reported careless handing-over by the British at the time of leaving India, with stores missing and funds in the public and non-public accounts untraceable. The remaining assets now had to be divided between the armed forces of the two countries at partition. This was compounded by the brand new, proud and hopeful Indian Government's thrust towards economic and social development. Defence spending was a low priority and the armed forces were in reduction mode. We had to make do with whatever had been left behind by the departing British. This included motorcycles, trucks and load carriers made by Enfield, Dodge, Chevrolet, Bedford, and tanks like Churchill, Sherman, Mark I and Mark II. Some of these had been to war and returned in damaged and run-down condition. With foreign exchange in extremely short supply, the only solution for the Indian army was to cannibalise and indigenise. Spares had to be fabricated locally to keep all this precious equipment functional.

Poona had a large number of army units and each had its own requirement for supplies. Besides the regiments which were stationed here, Poona also had the College of Military Engineering, Bombay Engineer Group & Centre, and various Ordnance Depots including the Central Vehicle Depots where vehicles were stored, serviced and polished down to the last spark plug, ready to swing into lightning action if war happened to break out.

Procurement was done centrally, and the process was highly organized. However, the local traders and small manufacturers, who might normally not have been considered as suitable vendors for the armed forces, were certainly eligible in this situation. Much of the growth of Poona trade and manufacture is related to this spurt in demand from the Defence in those days.

At that time, of course, I did not have the benefit of this historical perspective. By late 1953 my only concern was that our business had begun to plateau. I had a very clear sense that this market and this rate of growth would never be sufficient to fulfil the growing needs of our growing family.

I had settled into the family business, and through daily routine, managed to find some moments of adventure. I travelled around Poona as well as other cities such as Kolhapur and Solapur on collection duty. On one occasion, I remember we had supplied goods on credit to a glass works at Ogalewadi and there was an outstanding amount of Rs. 700. After a lot of reminders to which we received no reply, it was decided that I should go to Ogalewadi and collect the money. My friend Joglekar decided to accompany me. Our mission yielded a part payment in the form of a cheque for Rs. 200.

Rather than going straight back home, we decided to head for Goa which was not far away. On the way, we met two gentlemen from Bombay, so now there were four of us going to Goa.

Then, Goa was under Portuguese rule. It was a beautiful, clean place, with very little traffic and not many people to be seen on the streets. Panjim was an attractive and well-designed city. People were so honest that you could leave your bag at the bus station and when you came back at the end of the day it would still be there, untouched. One of our Bombay companions had a camera and he took photos at every opportunity. We marvelled at the churches, temples, beaches, buses and small old taxis in the city.

Late in the evening of our second day in Goa, a police inspector came to the hotel we were staying and requested us to accompany him to the police station.

Alarmed and wary of the harassment we might have to face, we went along, only to find that our fears were unfounded. The inspector cordially asked about our work, purpose of our visit, and so on. Joglekar and I gave our information and the two from Bombay said that they worked at a jewellery store. We told him that all of us were tourists in Goa. He then casually inquired why we had been taking so many photos. Sheepishly, our new friend handed over his camera, explaining that it was just a hobby. The inspector pulled out the roll, returned the camera, and allowed us to leave, which we did with great relief though a little embarrassed.

When we returned home after this pleasant break I was charged, even more than before, with the energy to break out and do something larger, with more potential. One idea that occurred to me was to begin supplying to the government. This would warrant us a dramatic increase in quantity. I was confident that I could supply large volumes of the highest quality required by the government.

I inquired about how one could qualify as an approved vendor for the government. I was informed that you had to first register your company, then submit a tender with your proposal for the requirement. In theory, all the sealed tenders would be collected and on the published date they would be opened, compared, and the most attractive proposal would be given the order.

Submitting a tender was a process that required lengthy and complicated paperwork. The first thing to be done was to find someone who could take care of this. Accordingly, I hired a part-time typist, Mr. Vaze. He would come to our shop in the evening, and from 6 to 8 p.m. daily he would be busy typing out the various applications and follow-up letters required. Mr. Vaze was a simple and kind-hearted man. A government employee himself, with vast experience in this type of documentation, he worked hard to educate me on these mysterious processes, and I worked hard to learn them.

We began the process of registering our company name and then started sending out proposals. For a long period our tenders were all rejected, but I persisted. After making inquiries, I learnt through various sources that the tender business did not depend on the most competitive price or even the standing and reputation of the supplier (although these were certainly important) but rather on one's network of contacts. If you knew the right person, you stood a better chance of having your tender accepted.

I now began to visit the government departments concerned, and spent time trying to cultivate those with the power to take decisions in my favour. The process was lengthy, tedious, and required continuous effort.

To register your company as a suitable vendor, you had to fill various forms, submit bank and tax documents and a sales track record. A physical inspection of the premises would then be made, after which your registration would be considered. Once registered, you were entitled to submit a tender. All these stages required continuous, repeated and wearying follow-up. My unflagging persistence did result in a few small orders after several months. But it was extremely difficult to get an entry. My elder brothers tried to dissuade me, feeling that it was beneath our dignity to put ourselves in a position where we had to bow down before anyone and keep asking for favours. I, however, was determined to break out of the small retail business and start working with large volumes. I could see before me an opportunity involving an investment of nothing more than a typewriter and a certain amount of legwork which I was more than willing to do. This could immediately result in increased business, higher turnover and extra profits. There was no way this kind of growth could come from just the shop!

For growth, one must continuously innovate. One must constantly observe customer requirements, changing habits and market trends. One must remain always at the forefront of discovery, understanding emerging technologies and always looking for lucrative ways in which to put them to use. I had learnt these principles through my observation and experience, and they have always remained at the core of my working methods.

As I was struggling with the tender business, I got an entry as a supplier to the Defence Services. As happened to me many times in my life, help came suddenly, swiftly, and from a totally unexpected source.

At one of my customer's shops, I bumped into a bearded man wearing a turban. I looked at him and smiled. It was rare to see a Sikh in this city. When I greeted him with, "Sat Sri Akal, Sardarji!" his native salutation, and proceeded to talk to him in his own language, he was equally delighted, and inquired how I could speak Punjabi so well. I told him of the time I had spent in Amritsar and this became an immediate bond between us.

He was Surinder Singh Sabarwal, a civilian supervisor at the 512 Army Base Workshop, who was to be a significant influence and guiding force in my life. He was trying to procure some electrical switches, and seemed frustrated because no vendor had yet submitted a tender for that particular design.

I immediately offered to acquire the items for him, and promptly submitted the documents required to register Ramchand Bhagwandas & Co. as a suitable supplier for the 512 Army Base Workshop. I applied myself to the tasks and soon enough, we had submitted the tender and once we received the approval, I procured the switches from Bombay and supplied them. We received our payment through an elaborate army procedure, submitting bills in the specified format, along with an inspection note. The payment would then be made through the Defence Pay & Accounts Department.

The 512 Army Base Workshop is a unit of the Corps of Electrical & Mechanical Engineers (EME), whose mandate is to achieve and maintain operational fitness of army equipment. The Workshop is located at Khadki, where the British had built a smaller cantonment to supplement the one at Poona. Tanks requiring repair would come from various parts of the country to this Workshop. Here they would be dismantled and each part inspected for wear and tear. Parts that needed replacement would have to be procured or fabricated.

Situated right next to the 512 Army Base Workshop was the CAFVD, the Central Armoured Fighting Vehicle Depot, where actual tanks were lined up ready to roll out and face the action. The CAFVD also held all the stock of fighting vehicle spare parts, with the records of the various models and their registration numbers stored meticulously. A separate registration was required for the CAFVD, and we went through the whole process again and yet again when dealing with the Central Ordnance Depot (COD) at Dehu Road.

We began to receive inquiries for products of different nomenclature and I became fully involved in supplying these requirements.

Very soon, I was making daily visits to these units, cycling once or twice every day between my home at Narayan Peth and Khadki, a distance of around six kilometres.

It took me three and a half to four hours to cycle from Naryan Peth to Dehu Road, a distance of around 25 km on the Bombay Poona road. The highway was a single-lane road with mostly cycle traffic, some motorcycles and a few cars. Large stretches were still mud road, yet to be asphalted. The ride got even bumpier as you turned off the highway to reach the COD. Cycling here every week was exhausting, but the excitement of entering a new field with seemingly unlimited prospects drove away my fatigue completely.

I soon learnt that the Indian Army has extremely strict quality control for its equipment. Every single specification must be conformed to, right down to the smallest detail. Defence production is highly specialized and complex. Each product must be safe, reliable, consistent in quality, and capable of operating under extreme conditions in various terrains and climates.

These strict quality requirements struck a chord in me. I understood, at a very deep level within myself, how important purity and genuineness were and this period of close interaction with the army procedures and controls consolidated these personal attributes. Though I was already well aware that customers will always be attracted by high quality, I now began to experience the delight of revelling in quality just for the sake of quality itself, regardless of the customer, and regardless of any circumstance.

Over the next few months, Sabarwalsaab and I became close friends. I visited his home and he visited mine along with his two children and met my mother and brothers. We were not from the same native area, but had much in common, both our families having fled our homeland because of partition.

He began to help me understand the parts of each item. He also helped me get permission from the commanding officer to take samples out of the Workshop so that I could have them replicated. He often provided me with elaborate drawings and descriptions of the technical specifications of each part.

I would first search the Bombay markets where one would sometimes come across these items unexpectedly. If unsuccessful there, I would come back to Poona and look around for a city workshop which could fabricate the sample for me. Here again was interesting work, with the additional challenge of ensuring that my supplier never came in direct contact with my customer and cut me out of the process. The only major difficulty now was the travel. I would have to cycle daily to Khadki and sometimes to Dehu Road, shuttling between these places and the workshops where the samples were being fabricated, in the process of making adjustments until the design was perfected. These workshops were scattered, and locating them meant searching carefully through each area of the city. They usually consisted of small dimly-lit open sheds or corner-rooms of one of the old wadas, with three or four people operating a lathe, drilling machine or welding machine, and doing other odd repair jobs for auto and oil engines. Our samples gave them something different to turn their hands to. Some would find them difficult to understand and refuse while others, intrigued, would be happy to try out something new which held a higher profit margin. Kishan would often sit and work alongside, taking the trouble to understand the workings of each mechanism. Right from this early beginning, our pattern was that he would work at the site of manufacture, while I worked for the business outside. In those days we had no conception or background of the distinctions between manufacturing, administrative, marketing and other business functions. We saw what was before us, and we did what we had to do. It was that simple.

Each product that we were given was unique, and invariably quite different from anything we had ever seen before. Each quotation would come in precise, military language using terms and figures and reference numbers and encryptions referring to the tanks, which I gradually became familiar with.

I would collect the sample, sometimes heavy or large and unwieldy, and carry it (often quite a long distance) to my cycle which I would have left tied to the stand outside the Army Workshop. I would then cycle the distance to the shop, and then spend the next few days hauling it around the city looking for someone willing to try to replicate it.

Most of the items were complex and unfamiliar. It was usually difficult to find a workshop which would agree to do it. We would then have to supervise the process and keep improvising until we had a perfect replica of the sample that had been given to us. Some products required that a mould be first prepared. Sometimes we would need to get permission to dissect the sample since nobody could imagine what was inside! All this cost money but we never grudged it, knowing that they were not frivolous expenses but business costs.

This was definitely exciting, stimulating work. We went through this process with dozens of different products, getting each one made at a different fabrication unit.

Kishan had now begun working with me, and participated in this activity with great enthusiasm. It was during this time, as we began to fabricate these items, that we gradually realised that it would be possible for us to manufacture the goods ourselves.

I remember one order I executed for five hundred army truck silencers. We received the sample and drawings from the COD Dehu Road. Kishan prepared the sample with the help of a welder near the Sarbatwala Chowk in the Poona Camp area. It had to be approved by the TDEV Ahmednagar. But it was the COD Dehu Road which had the authority to issue the order, and this came only after continuous follow-up. For this, I made innumerable trips on my bicycle from Narayan Peth to Dehu Road. Travelling to Ahmednagar was another big effort.

I would get into the ancient, rickety State Transport bus at the Swargate depot in Poona at 7.15 a.m. It was a five-hour journey to Ahmednagar. The bus would be filled with village folk on their way home after a shopping trip, carrying city supplies for their families.

The TDEV Ahmednagar was around 15 km from the city bus depot. Once there I would have to negotiate a price with the tongawala before we set off on the long, bumpy and dusty ride ahead.

In those days, if you were thirsty, you had to look for a roadside tap or a tube-well hand pump. Food was not a priority for me. Since my early working days I had got quite used to going hungry or being fed leftovers and scraps. I was able to tolerate the taste and texture of the lumpy dal and leathery chapattis in the army dining halls where I was sometimes kindly allowed to have a meal. While travelling, there were no roadside dhabas in these areas and I would make do with chai and peanuts or maybe a banana or two if I was lucky. Today, the Poona-Nagar road is fast turning into a broad highway with reckless traffic, fancy eating places and even shopping centres, quite different from the lonely dirt road it used to be.

The TDEV office closed at 4 p.m. and all outsiders would be ordered to leave on the dot of time. Quite often the work I had come for would still be pending. I would very often head back for Poona, only to return to Nagar next day to complete my task. On the journey home, I would be accompanied on the State Transport bus by farmers heading into town to sell their produce. The samples I was carrying back to replicate would have sacks of grain, baskets of squawking chicken, and long, wide jute bags of potatoes and leafy vegetables for company.

I remember one incident when we received a large order through the DGS&D which was to be supplied on a specific date. The sample had been approved by TDEV Ahmednagar, and the local CAFVD office would now have to inspect the goods before we sealed and supplied them. We worked frantically as the last date approached. Very soon, there were only two days left, and finally only one. We worked all night, with my friend Sabarwal and his team helping us to assemble and pack the product, ready for supply. Finally by 5 o'clock in the morning, we were ready with everything laid out for the inspection. We had not slept for two nights in a row.

I remember the satisfied delight of the officer, Captain Urs, who came to conduct the inspection. Partly it was because the goods were desperately needed and were of good quality and partly because we had laid them out so neatly and within the specified time limit. His trust in our quality by now was such that he knew it was not necessary for him to inspect each and every single piece before he accepted our shipment.

During this period of my life, I never stopped moving. Travel was continuous. I would wake early morning and set off, and keep moving until late at night when I would fall asleep, exhausted, only to wake and start again next morning.

When I think about it now, I realise that there was some driving force moving me, guiding me, helping me to take quick decisions. At that time, all that I had in me was the conviction that there was a job before me, and I had to complete it.

I now began to extend my reach, and travelled to Army Workshops and Depots in other parts of the country as well-Meerut, Agra, Bangalore, Delhi and others. We had registered separately at each of these places, going through the lengthy process of filling forms, showing proof of work done at the 512 Army Base Workshop in Poona and so on. To get all these permissions and to have the various samples approved, I had to make innumerable trips to Delhi.

With each order we completed, the profits would come in, and I would feel the satisfaction of having my decisions vindicated, and seeing my business grow. All the trouble and effort would then seem inconsequential.

Though this was difficult and uphill work, I could sense that it was superior to selling electrical accessories in a shop.

Each sample was listed in the army base in an enormous directory with a code name and a 12-digit serial number. Just the name alone would have been confusing enough for me. It was a new world, and every step of it brought learning.

Most of these were high-security items, and there was considerable paperwork required to get permission to take them outside the army premises. I would spend the entire day, or sometimes a few days, in going through this process.

I would carefully remove any label or identifying mark on the sample which could reveal to whom I was supplying, and would naturally never disclose to the fabricators who my customer was. If anyone tried to question me I would pretend that the consignment was being sent to some vague but important customer in Delhi or another city. Though each order was for a small number of parts, the margins were excellent. Each of these items was of high value, but did not cost much to make. A simple auto cable with terminals welded at two ends was considered an excellent deal at Rs. 10 per piece by the COD. No one had any way of knowing that it had cost only Rs. 2 to make.

The biggest lesson I learnt during this period was that manufacturing was where the real profits lay. The cost of raw material would always be relatively limited and a small percentage of the total price. Overhead costs too would be distributed over volumes, and in fact our overheads did not amount to much. We were paying no rent or salaries. We did not use packaging materials but delivered our goods wrapped in book-binding paper. Even our personal expenses were low. But the price you could get for your ingenuity, for the value that you added to your own product, would all go straight into your pocket, and this was the key difference between manufacturing and trading.

In addition to this most important lesson, the entire period was one of overall growth and learning for me. Steeped in the army environment of regimentation and discipline, the work values that I had always carried within me became compounded. I found this environment excellent and highly enjoyable. I began to learn the documentation and procedures. Quotations and forms came in stilted army language, which I began to get accustomed to. In this environment, I also started becoming familiar with spoken English.

In 1953, the NDA, our National Defence Academy, the first indigenous Indian Defence training institute and a matter of great national pride, was being constructed and Kishan helped the company which received the contract to lay the electrical wiring. People still remember his total involvement, climbing poles and supervising the laying of wires for this prestigious institute.

I continued my commitment to increasing the volumes of goods we were trading in, but I now knew that we had to find a way to begin manufacturing the goods we were supplying.

As volumes grew, so did profits. I now began executing orders for Rs. 50,000 and for even a lakh of rupees. However, I still had no grip on how the money was being used. All I could see was that I was bringing in bigger and bigger business.

By 1954, the volumes had grown and it was now necessary for me to register with the DGS&D, the Directorate General of Supplies & Disposals, situated at Shah Jehan Road in Delhi. This was the highest authority for Defence procurement, and all big tenders across the country were centralised here. Once you were registered with the DGS&D, it meant that you had been approved by the Finance Ministry, and there was no limit to the tender value you could submit.

To break into this elite circle of suppliers, I had to fill a form and begin a long process of waiting my turn and continuously following up to check the status.

Government officials were always busy and never valued a businessman's time. I believe this continues to be the case even today. There were many occasions on which I would travel to Delhi with a confirmed appointment, be made to wait all day, and then be rudely informed that the person who was to meet me was too busy. After waiting the next day as well, I would go back home where my work waited. There would be times when I would hand over my business card and the person it was given to would take one look at it and fling it aside in disgust or tear it up and throw it away in my presence. But I never stopped trying. I would make sure I made another trip within a few days and somehow manage to meet the person who had promised me his time. Despite all the obstructions, it never once struck me that it was difficult, or that I couldn't do it. All my energy was focussed towards overcoming every obstacle and getting the job done. The trips to Delhi became monthly, often twice or thrice a month, even weekly at times. I was a regular commuter on the Frontier Mail and I became familiar with every railway station on the Bombay-Delhi. A large percentage of my time was spent travelling and waiting at the government offices or Army Workshops in Delhi.

All the while, I never stopped looking for means to connect with the right person who would help me to get my job done. Looking back, I can see how much I learnt about how to deal with different types of people, and how to get things done in different ways and quickly switch from one approach to another depending on the situation. All this energy spent in looking for loopholes to cut through the bureaucratic process now seems like a terrible waste of productive time. However, that was the phase of development our country was going through and every entrepreneur like me, who had aspirations but no background of money or personal contacts, had no choice but to undergo it.

Eventually, I began to receive the large orders I was struggling to get. But this led to a new hurdle. My elder brothers were uncomfortable with the new quantities. I remember the first manufacturing order I received was worth Rs. 3 lakhs.

I had applied for a tender to lay a flat copper braiding on the cables used in tanks. We had been working with harness assemblies, and Kishan had become an expert on wiring them.

A wiring harness assembly is a complete electrical wiring system for a vehicle. We put together these assemblies for trucks, tanks and other army vehicles. The harness ensures perfect coordination between all the electrical parts of the vehicle, from the brake lights at the back, to ignition, dashboard, front lights and so on. The wires are routed through special cavities in the vehicle. The harness assembly is a compact and beautifully designed unit which can be lifted out of and replaced into the vehicle for easy maintainability. This particular tender required that the cable, which was thick corrugated hose made of galvanised iron, be covered in copper braiding to earth it.

The approval was delivered to me by post from the DGS&D. I opened the envelope and when I saw what it contained, I experienced a shock of delight.

In excitement and gratitude, I raced at once to Surinder Singh Sabarwal, the man who had made all this possible for me, helping and guiding me in both Poona and Delhi. He was equally elated, and sent for my elder brothers. They both liked and respected him and came at once. But when he gave them the good news, they were aghast. They told me that I must have lost my mind to imagine that we could execute delivery of that size. All we had was Rs. 30,000, and that was engaged in the business. "Do you know how many zeros there are in three lakhs!" they laughed, since I was rather famous for my lack of education. They honestly believed that because we did not have liquidity to that tune, we would be unable to supply the goods.

That night I was unable to sleep, alternately fuming and crying, desperately wondering how I could proceed. Hardly ever in my life have I experienced the kind of frustration I felt that night. Today I understand that my brothers had experienced financial ruin and disgrace at an early age and it had made them cautious and terrified of the smallest element of risk. But at that time, I felt stifled by them, and was filled with anger. None of my brothers had ever visited any of the Army Workshops or Depots or even the DGS&D in Delhi. Our largest source of income was the Defence supply business, for which I who was solely responsible. However, Kishan gave me his full support. He had experienced the flow of the business and knew what a fantastic opportunity this was for us.

Now with the Rs. 3 lakh order for copper braided cables, and with Kishan's support, the time had come. We decided that we would go ahead and buy a copper braiding machine. We knew that this was available from Japan, and we ordered it immediately through the import agents Batliboi & Co. The machine cost us our entire savings from the business so far. I now had to worry about our operational costs.

I knew from my past experience with shops and through my collection activities that money could be procured through various sources. It would have been very easy for me to go to a traditional moneylender, write a hundi, and take as much as I wanted. But I knew very well that this was a habit that could destroy you. There was much more discipline in borrowing from a bank.

However, I had no idea where to start. There was no one to whom I could turn for advice. I had some experience of working with banks because of my job with the Sakhranis. One day I noticed that a new bank had come up near our office. This was the Central Bank of India's new Poona branch, situated on Lakshmi Road. I decided to enter and try my luck.

The manager Mr. Mobedji greeted me, examined my documents respectfully and listened with interest to my request. He suggested that I visit their head office in Bombay and meet their General Manager Mr. Patel for his sanction.

Mr. Patel chatted with me about my unit. He told me that he liked the idea that India could now make cables that were formerly only imported. He asked me how much I needed. I confided to him that if I was to expand the way I really wanted to, I would need Rs. 5 lakh. He thought for a moment and then said to me that he would agree to an immediate sanction of Rs. 3 lakh. "Two reasons," he said. "One – you are a Sindhi. Two – I have seen your track record. I know I will get all my money back, with interest."

I received a letter the very next day – turn-around time unheard of in the present day. We had been authorized cash credit against bills raised as well as an amount for the purchase of capital goods towards expansion.

We opened an account which required signatures of all four brothers. We send the signed letter, received an advance and we were ready to start operations. All our bills now began to be rotated through the bank. Since that day my company has enjoyed credit facilities, a resource which we have cultivated and used carefully.

Despite how busy we were or occupied or stressed with other matters, the bank date was never overstepped on; not even a single occasion.

Companies sometimes feel that they are losing only a small amount of extra interest when they miss a date of repayment. This is not true, because when you miss a date you are losing your credibility as well. Even if you pay your due amount two weeks later, you will never enjoy the same kind of trust as someone who always pays on time. It's no use trying to explain your problems to the bank. This doesn't concern them in the least, and only serves to create a poor impression. When you have an agreement, never try to change it half-way. This discipline of repaying on time gave us a solid credit history, which gave my company one of its most important intangible assets and later became the foundation for our exponential growth.

Neither Kishan nor I had the slightest idea of cost or space requirements, installation issues or any fundamental aspect of running a manufacturing business. Today anyone thinking of setting up a small-scale industry (SSI) would – and must – do thorough homework on cost projections, market opportunities, and various studies of feasibility.

None of these things was even on the periphery of our consciousness. We were ignorant and uneducated. Besides, it was a completely virgin market – and a protected one at that. We saw the opportunity, felt enthusiasm in our minds and hearts and went ahead and did it. It was just a natural flow of events. I think back on those days with some amount of amusement, incredulity and pride. I also think that it may not be possible for anyone in today's complicated, competitive, fast-paced world to do what we did. Without planning, a genuine in-depth understanding of industry and proper comprehension of technology and processes, nobody could bumble along and set up an industry from scratch as we did.

With the new large order in hand and our new machine, we began to look for a place where we could begin to run our first venture, and soon rented a small space in Kakakuwa Mansion on Lakshmi Road which was once used as a cowshed. It was a small open shed with a corrugated iron roof and a thickly-packed cowdung floor. The cows were gone, but their smell remained.

We were very proud of our beautiful new Japanese machine but unfortunately none of us had the slightest clue about how it was to be installed and used. The manual that came with the machine had some unhelpful diagrams and Kanji characters which made no sense whatever to us and we went about getting hints from anyone in the city who knew a little Japanese. Kishan had many friends who like him were technically inclined, and they, spent days together working on the machine, often sleeping at the on site. Someone said at first that for such a heavy machine why should we waste money building a foundation? So we brought a truckload of sand and laid the machine on it. But it would not work. We then had to clear away all the sand and make a foundation after all. This was just one of the many mistakes we made. This was the first machine of its kind that Batliboi had imported into India and we got some help from them as well.

Finally, Kishan's attempts at reverse engineering were successful. One of the friends who had helped install the machine was A.G. Joshi who had a well-equipped mechanical workshop. One of Mr. Joshi's biggest achievements in later years was the work he did for Philips to develop shadowless lamps, which could be used in operating theatres and laboratories. He had a highly advanced mechanical talent, and Kishan had learnt a lot from him. He told us that there were units in Poona manufacturing nada (cotton tape), using Japanese machines from the same company; the Kokuban Iron Works. It turned out that these machines performed an identical process! We first understood the working of those machines and then we could make good progress on our machine.

Besides learning how to operate the machine, we also began to learn other essentials of business such as LCs or letters of credit, pro-forma invoices and how to talk to people from other parts of the country or abroad. Important messages had to be sent and received by telegram and we soon learnt to use and understand their abbreviated sentences and coded punctuation.

To make the wire, raw copper had to be tinned- a process which was done in hot baths and then drawn into wires. Surat, the home of masters of artificial jewellery, was a centre for this activity and we ordered large quantities of the copper, which was delivered to us in huge bobbins. It took us a while to realise that these bobbins were far too large to use in the operations! The first thing we would have to do was rewind multiple numbers of wires onto smaller bobbins. These could then be placed inside the machine and the wire would be fed in as a ribbon and would get braided.

We had bought the machine, rented space, and installed it. It had not struck us that we needed to design a workshop for a range of related activities. As we began manufacturing, we realised that, every day there was some shifting or adjustment to be made. Every day we came across new requirements or processes that had previously skipped our attention. It was all very interesting, with many surprises and a great deal of learning.

Finally, we had produced a sample and were ready for it to be inspected by our end users, the Indian Army. The officials arrived in army vehicles and full dress uniform, the senior stepping out to smart salutes of his subordinates. They entered our little cowshed, raising eyebrows and shooting looks of surprise and concern at each other. However, our product passed muster and they were delighted since braided copper wire was a very urgent requirement at that time and they must have decided to overlook the cowdung floor in favour of product quality.

It strikes me today that it must surely have been possible for us to get a better location for the factory that was to launch us as businessmen. But we were so ignorant, and had so little exposure that we just settled for the first place that was shown to us. The people we knew tended to set up their places of business right inside their wadas, breaking a door or a wall facing the main road, and continuing to live alongside.

Kishan and I worked hard to execute the order which was not only delivered on time but brought us a profit of Rs. one lakh, an enormous sum of money for the time.

My days of travelling by bicycle were now finally over! Overcoming some resistance from our elder brothers, Kishan and I bought ourselves an old second-hand British Trump motorcycle, which cut down the time to Khadki to just 10 minutes and to Dehu Road to just half an hour.

We now had two flourishing businesses, retail and manufacturing, and we decided to set up a separate company for the manufacturing activity.

The new manufacturing unit was registered as a partnership company, Indian Cable Industries. My elder brothers continued to be equal partners and it was an unstated fact that, being seniors, their decisions would prevail. However, I now had operational control, and this was exhilarating for me. Another advantage we had was that the bank saw our turnover increase and our balances rise, confidence in our abilities grew and our credit facilities consolidated.

We continued working in this way, managing both our shop Ramchand Bhagwandas & Co. and also our new manufacturing company Indian Cable Industries, though I was no longer personally involved in the shop. Both continued to flourish and grow. All of us brothers were now earning well and could afford to indulge ourselves in occasional holidays. In 1956, I accompanied my friend Thakur to Kashmir. We travelled for several days through spectacularly beautiful scenery and stayed in a 2 bedroomed shikara on the lake in Srinagar. When Thakur's wife came from Bombay to join him, I set off on my own, making friends along the way.

The pace of life was quite different from what it is today. Today we squeeze an entire holiday into weekends and when people travel, they find three or four days quite enough to feel that they know and understand a place. But back then, people used to set off on long journeys and stay in one comfortable holiday spot, or at a place of pilgrimage, for weeks at a time, spending the entire day just sitting and enjoying the scenery, or in worship, listening to discourses or singing bhajans together, or taking long walks, and conversing companionably with strangers. I made a friend, Mohan Mahajan, a young man of about my age from Amritsar, and we spent a few days riding around Pahalgam on our hired ponies, and eating the excellent food served by roadside dhabas. From Pahalgam, noticing the large numbers of pilgrims on their way to the holy cave shrine of Amarnath, I decided to join them, and hired a pony.

We noticed a large number of pilgrims passing through Pahalgam on their way to the holy shrine of Amarnath, a cave which attracts thousands of devotees to its natural ice formation in the shape of a Shiva Lingam. Two ice formations on either side representing Parvati, wife of Shiva and Ganesh, their son. Since Mohan backed out, I joined a band of about twenty people and began the journey. The first stage of the trek is to Chandanwadi, the second to Sheshnag Lake and the third over the Mahagunas Pass to Panchtarni from where one can walk to the cave.

This was one of the most scenic journeys I had ever seen. Beautiful villages on the way and clear views of mountains, the entire journey through a landscape of pine forests, mountains treams, hills and valley is truly breathtaking. Since I was totally unprepared and inappropriately dressed for such altitude, others in our group helped me with clothes, blankets and sheets. Though we were all strangers, there was a warmth and family feeling that I still remember.

That night, shivering in the unfamiliar cold, I stepped out of the tent to look at the beautiful, awe-inspiring mountains in the moonlight.

I stood still for some moments, looking out at the beautiful Sheshnag Lake on one side and the mountains on the other. Perhaps the mountains also have a voice! I thought to myself, and I asked them the question that was always on my mind. What will be my future? Will I grow from here? Will I continue to be a small trader?

To my surprise, there was an immediate answer. You will grow very fast and very big in industry. Be patient and wait! In time you will see how big you will grow.

I came back and slept, reassured. But in the morning when we got up there was heavy rain. It would be impossible to continue the climb in the difficult road through these heavy rains. Some of us decided to return, and reached Pahalgam late at night.

I came back to Poona, secure with the answer from the mountains giving me comfort to face the struggle ahead.

Our business was growing well and in 1958, Kishan and I heard some exciting news. The government was organizing a World Trade Fair in Delhi. Industries from other countries had been invited to display their products. Indian companies too would be participating.

In the late 1950s, with India's focus on industrial development, one of the grounds in Delhi was taken over and converted into a huge industrial mela. It was later named Pragati Maidan, and continues to be the venue of the biggest trade and industrial exhibitions in this country, attracting more and more buyers and visitors every year.

In 1958, the exhibition was well advertised by the government, and generated a fervour of enthusiasm and curiosity. People like us came from all over the country to visit. The largest number of visitors came from local crowds, with residents of Delhi and the nearby areas strolling into the exhibition grounds to inspect and marvel at the new advances in technology.

In today's age of lightning communication and technology, it's hard to remember that in the late 1950s, machines were something new and marvellous. Our country had always been rich in raw material, and the British had exploited these riches, shipping out liberal quantities to feed various manufacturing processes in their country, and shipping back ready-made goods to sell in our growing, captive market. The large industrialists had capital and other resources. But this was the first time in our history that people like us could dream of enterprise on such a scale. Walking through the aisles of the exhibition ground, one could sense an excitement in the crowd. I'm sure that Kishan and I were not the only ones whom the environment infected with the fire of entrepreneurship!

We were fascinated to come across a small plastic extruding machine. The agents representing this product were H.S. Shobha Singh & Sons. With this machine, input of plastic could extrude ready-made plastic cable, rods, tubes, or pipes.

We knew we had to buy this line for ourselves. In a ferment of excitement, we discussed the matter with our elder brothers and they were equally enthusiastic. Without a second thought, we decided to put down Rs. 15,000 cash and ordered the machine from Germany.

We were staying at my favourite haunt in Delhi, the Sindh Punjab Hotel which faced the railway station and where rooms were available for Rs. 3.50 per night. This was where I continued to stay on my visits to Delhi, for many years to come.

On the side of the road, a typist sat near the tram line, preparing applications of various kinds. People needed ration cards, licenses and those like us, without office infrastructure of their own, needed to prepare many kinds of documents.

I had to submit an application for an import licence for our beautiful extrusion machine. On that cold January morning, I wrote this with some help from the typist, since he had much more experience than I did with documents of this nature. He showed me the format of someone else's pro-forma application, and we gratefully followed its guidance.

I then took it to the office of the Chief Controller of Imports & Exports (CCIE) which was located on Shah Jahan Road and not at Udyog Bhavan as it is today. I submitted it to the clerk at the desk, one Gurcharan Singh, and without as much as an upward glance he stamped and cleared it.

A few years later, machine import procedure became complicated and still later all imports were banned completely. Since we had made it by the proverbial whisker, I was sure the fates were unmistakably on my side!

PVC, or polyvinyl chloride, was a new material, First produced commercially in the U. S., in the early 1930s, it became widespread and found many applications after World War II, especially as an ideal material for cable insulation. The war had resulted in shortage of natural materials such as rubber and cotton. Scientists had produced synthetic resins and fibres made from easily-available petrochemical material to take their place. PVC had a natural advantage over rubber, it could withstand rigorous weathering and last for fifty years and more!

In 1959, India was importing PVC cables from Germany and England. Till now, Indian cable manufacturers had been producing only rubber cables and all the PVC cables were imported. With our machine, we would be the first to produce PVC cables in this country! It was a thrilling thought.

It was time for us to move out of the little cowshed at Kakakuwa mansion at Lakshmi Road. We now began looking for a better place and finally set up our factory at the site of Udhyam Engineering on Karve Road, on rent. The owner happened to be the brother of Nathuram Godse, the assassin of Mahatma Gandhi. After Gandhi's death, they had been continuously harassed and unable to run their business. We took over the place at a rent of Rs. 1200 per month.

The other day I was driving past this area where our first proper factory had been and found everything totally changed. Though the old church still remains at the same spot, I couldn't help remembering the old days when I would ride home slowly and carefully from here because there was not a single street light. It was completely and unnervingly dark. How different it is now, brightly lit and bustling with intense activity.

Once again when the machine arrived, we went through a long process of adjustments and learning. Once again Kishan took help from his friends and they worked day and night to install the machine. He was newly married at this time, but he was so involved with setting it up that many days he would work late into the night, falling off to sleep at the factory and starting work again first thing in the morning. By now he had become expert in the technology of all the products we were dealing in and related products as well, an expertise that he was to develop and excel in for the next half century and more.

Our new extruder required supporting machinery. We ordered wire line and wire drawing machines from Surat. We also had a coiling machine fabricated. Other downside equipment was purchased or designed accordingly.

Our new technology was such a great novelty, and generated so much interest in the manufacturing community that Mr. Abasaheb Garware, today recognized as doyen of the Indian plastics industry visited us. He marvelled at our factory and discussed our plans for running it - something we were ourselves then not very clear about!

Our Karve Road factory had nine employees. One or two of them had some mechanical experience and aptitude. But most of them were just youngsters whom Kishan had to train right from scratch. He had a very good relationship with his team. They would come to work at around 8.30 and continue till around 6.30 in the evening and on days when there was extra work they stayed on with enthusiasm, without a trace of resentment, to complete it. We would order food from outside and eat it together. We worked together like one family.

Our suppliers of PVC resin for the machine were the Imperial Chemical Industry (ICI) headquartered in Calcutta. Recognizing our handicap and aware that we would soon be one of their big customers, they offered to train Kishan on PVC applications. They had a model of a machine similar to ours, and Kishan spent two weeks at their Calcutta Tiljalla Laboratory learning all they could teach him.

We also had help from our friend Vasantrao Vaidya of Swastik Rubber Products Limited. All this while, we had been buying rubber cables from him and selling them under our brand. Vaidya was skilled in technology, a very good person, and a true friend to us. Some months after we had imported our extrusion machine, we needed a small spare part from Germany. By this time there were import restrictions. We would have had to wait for three or four months to receive the part, during which time the machine would have been lying idle and our orders and expenses piling up. Mr. Vaidya happened to be going to Germany on a business trip and brought the part for us in less than ten days, carrying it through customs in his coat pocket. In those days it was a daring act that only a true friend and well-wisher would do for you.

A few years later, he set up a PVC cable manufacturing plant of his own, and supplied cable to us which we sold under our own brand. He had started out manufacturing as well as selling, but soon realised that we had sold a far greater amount of his cables than he had. After all, selling was our forte. In the mid-1960s, when he saw our success at manufacturing and distributing cables all over the country, he transferred his entire cable machinery, raw material quota, and a portion of his plant to us.

In 1959, all set with space, machinery, orders, and working capital, our small-scale industry was ready to roll. However, this was not a simple matter! We had to register and we then would to be allotted a licence against which our quota of raw material would be issued. All imports were controlled by the government. Every Indian manufacturer would be allotted a licence for a certain amount, based on the size of the company, its infrastructure, and orders on hand. It was well known that what was more important than any of these formalities, was who you knew,which strings to pull with decision markers so as to get your quota increased. For those in the small-scale sector, the situation was bleak.

It was difficult to understand all the formalities involved, and also the huge amounts of paperwork required. I now hired a full-time typist, Mr. U. S. Anikhandi, who was to work with us for many years until his retirement, and naturally became known by the affectionate nickname "USA". We also employed a lady, Mrs. Pushpa Bopatkar, who served as accountant and billing in-charge.

We took care to show every application or document we prepared to an external expert who would vet and help us correct it. Similarly, we got all the communications we sent out checked and corrected. Those who helped us in this way were our friends and well-wishers and they fulfilled the function of today's highly-paid consultants with grace and kindness, but with no charge whatever.

The Licence Raj, as it used to be called, was a breeding ground for corruption. Though the government had very good intentions in spreading the thin supply of raw material to as many manufacturers as possible, the truth was that you could always buy raw material in the open market. There were always individuals and organizations who acquired their licences by illicit means, bought the raw material at government prices, and sold it at a premium to manufacturers who were desperate for it.

As long as the demand for our goods and our production capacity exceeded our licence quota of raw material, we really had no choice but to buy from the open market.

In today's world, the phrase "open market" has a cheerful ring to it and denotes a healthy environment of free trade and mutual prosperity. But in the controlled economy of the time, our "open market" consisted of goods sold illegally. The phrase indicated the lurking danger of contraband material that was often spurious and sold by disreputable sources. Desperate to fulfill our commitments and stay in the business, we bought from them.

At the same time, we kept up a continuous process of requesting, begging, demanding, pleading through letters, applications, meetings, and many number of placating measures to have our quota increased.

Poona had an Assistant Director of Industry, who would inspect our factory, our bank records, and other business information at regular intervals. We had to declare the type of machines we had and how much we produced daily, monthly and annually. We would then go through the process of filling forms and receive our registration number, after which we were eligible to apply for raw material. There were separate applications for copper and PVC. Once their Poona office was satisfied, our case would be directed to Bombay, to the office of the Development Commissioner, Directorate of Industry. A long period of document exchange, accompanied by all kinds of referrals and follow-up, would then ensue. Bombay had the authority to issue only small quantities. For higher licence values, we would be referred to Delhi, to the office of the Chief Controller for Imports & Exports. After the approval finally came from the CCIE, we would have to return to Bombay to collect our licence.

This process of continuous application and supplication would take around six months, at the end of which we would be issued a licence for material which would last us less than a month. Since we could only apply twice a year, there would be a long wait after which we would start the application process all over again. With this cycle, growth was excruciatingly slow. I spent a large portion of my time between Poona, Bombay, and Delhi, trying to explain to everyone who had any authority to help me that our licence quota for 1.5 tonnnes of PVC resin and 1 tonne of copper was just a tiny fraction of what our machine could handle, and far less than the demand I knew the market potentially held. I showed the letter to Gurcharan Singh, the government officer in Delhi, trying to explain my predicament and requesting him to help me to get the quota raised.

He tossed the letter back at me, cursing, in ripest Punjabi, the fool who had allowed me to import this machine into the country in the first place. If I hadn't been so frustrated, I would have smiled. He was the same official by whose grace the machine had been allowed into the country. He seemed to have forgotten me, an insignificant seeker of favours the like of whom he saw dozens every day. But to me he was an important man whom I could never forget.

While waiting for the licensed quota to be delivered, every red-blooded businessman was faced with the choice of leaving their machinery idle, or finding other means of procuring raw material. There was no method we didn't try. Sometimes we would get copper bars from Bombay, and this required a separate process of rolling to turn them into wire. Quite often, we bought raw material on the open market. Running our factory turned out to need much more money than we could have previously imagined. There were so many things that were required, sometimes motors of different sizes, or equipment for some unknown process or other. We learnt for the first time the cost of investing in your own product.

For nearly a year after we set up our SSI at Karve Road, the cost of our operations was supported by the Defence contracts. However, this involved immense paperwork, and almost daily travel between our factory, Khadki and Dehu Road.

Even then, the sheer quantity of work kept me away from the core business which I wanted to grow, and build my own products. By around the end of 1959, I decided that I would have to cut down the amount of time and effort I was spending on the Defence contracts and devote myself to my own manufacturing operations. We had some brand-new innovative and highly lucrative products which we had to introduce into the market, and we had to keep working to source more and more. These products were extremely successful not just in industry but for the Defence contracts as well.

One of our biggest breaks came from Kishan's study of automobile wire, which led to our taking up the manufacture of PVC auto cable. This became one of our most successful products, widely sold, eagerly awaited by the consumers, laying the ground for our reputation as innovative manufacturers.

Cables are of many different types. Unlike other products like, biscuits or motorcycles which perform one basic function, with changes giving rise to different features, cables are used for widely varying applications even when they look identical from the outside. Within the home, the type of electrical cable used for fan, radio, and refrigerator is completely different from the type of cable which connects the engine of an automobile to its lights, horn, and batteries. To transmit radio waves, aerial cables which vary in construction and design are used. The carrying capacity of each one is different, allowing varying voltages to pass through them. I brought all the different types of cables to our shop and Kishan would open them up to study their design.

In those days, all electrical cables were sheathed in rubber. This made them much thicker than they are today. The concept of concealed wiring was unknown. The wires would be laid on a baton of wood. Small strips of wood would be used to clip the wire to the wall. Each clip would be neatly spaced at a uniform distance of six or eight inches from the previous one. After a few years, the rubber would begin to crack, the cable would begin to lose its insulation, there would be risk of leakage, and the wiring would have to be replaced.

In the early days, automobile cable manufacturers would insulate the wires with rubber. However, rubber is sensitive and the oil and moisture to which it was constantly exposed to, would soften it, and the insulation would soon wear away. To prevent this from happening, they began to cover the rubber cable with a cotton braiding. Cotton on its own could not withstand moisture or oil, so the fabric would be further coated with a synthetic lacquer material that filled the interstices of the cotton making it resistant to oil and water, and thus impermeable. All this made manufacturing a slow and expensive process. Since lacquer too would soon rub off, the life of the cable was short.

When we replaced the rubber insulation with PVC, which is impervious to oil and water, the new PVC cable that we introduced not only occupied much less space than the bulky rubber one, it was also much longer lasting.

At this juncture, we learnt something new, useful, and extremely interesting about the consumer mindset. People were simply not accustomed to cable that looked and felt like this. Wiremen were familiar with wires covered with a thick jacket of rubber. Wire with a single layer of insulation was considered gimmicky, unsafe and unacceptable. Users were suspicious of the new product. Our auto cables too faced resistance from garage owners who ran a lucrative business changing wires frequently. However, progress can never be halted and we went into production.

With an eye on market need, for several months we actually insulated the PVC material and braided it with cotton, coating it with multiple coats of thin varnish to make it resemble the auto cable people were used to! Once the product stabilised, we were able to dispense with the extra process.

After good success in the market, we wrote to the ISI, the Indian Standards Institute (now known as the Bureau of Indian Standards) to approve this new method of making cable by replacing rubber with PVC insulation and listing its advantages, since at that time the approved standard was only rubber insulation.

Kishan and I continued with our already established roles. He was responsible for product development, factory operations and manufacturing, while my areas were procurement, administration, finance, selling and collection. Our elder brothers had preferred to continue handling the shop. Our youngest brother, Narayan, had completed his schooling and entered engineering college. However, after one year there he discontinued his education, and joined the shop. Narayan's decision to do this was not challenged by anyone. When I think back, it strikes me that if only our father had been alive, he would never have allowed this to happen. But we were all completely immersed in our work with hardly a moment to spare for our own comfort or each other's.

Kishan was constantly on the lookout for new technical information from magazines and from other companies. I did understand the process of manufacture, but definitely not at the level of detail that he did. In any case, I was busy with the other aspects of the business. We made an excellent team.

While on one side the government rules made procurement difficult, selling was equally hard because we had to compete with imported goods. Indian products were not well thought of. Poona dealers were hesitant, and in Bombay too I had only limited success. The very same Bombay vendors from whom I used to buy cable for my Defence requirement, and with whom I had established excellent working relationships, now avoided my visits because they were unwilling to risk stocking and promoting my cable against an international brand.

I began travelling all over the country to introduce my cable to distributors, a period of rough and almost continuous travel that continued well into the 1960s.

There were a number of old foreign cable companies which were highly respected. When I went around offering my product, I was met with completely cold response. However, I knew this game; I had played it before, and once again I employed the timeless sales strategies of trying again, and again, and again – the art of patient follow-up! It was tedious, and it was tough, but for me that was the only way to grow and I enjoyed doing it and seeing the results roll out before me.

Our beautiful new cable had to have a name. I sat together with my brothers, brainstorming possible names. The two adjectives that best described our product, we felt, were Fine and Flexible. Rolling them into one, the brand Finolex was born. It was just a word made up of the attributes we wanted for our product, nothing to do with a place or a family or anything like that. In fact, we could even have picked up the name of any other brand or company and called ourselves Mercedes Benz or Harrods if we had wanted to. But as it turned out, our name was simple and straightforward and describes us as well today as it did in 1958.

With all my travelling, I soon realised that distributors in the South were much more receptive and open to evaluating my product for its quality rather than just looking at my name or background, because they recognized value and showed interest in the product. Over the next few years, there was not a single town in South India that I did not visit, personally meeting dealers and distributors and acquainting them with the merits of my cable.

Travel was quite different from what it is now. The roads were rough and the vehicles in bad shape. The roadside eating joints served food of a quality that would today be shunned by even the poorest. There were no trade directories to which I could refer for names and addresses of establishments which would consider my products. These establishments were scattered all over. Though English was widely spoken and understood, these businessmen would use languages that I was never to learn, though in the course of those years some of the words did become familiar to me.

While travelling, it was my objective to appoint dealers who would represent my company and through whom I could supply material to their area. The first big break came when the renowned TVS group took up the agency for our PVC auto cables. It was a new product for them, and they took it on with enthusiasm.

Established in 1911 as a transport bus service, TVS had grown to a large provider of automobile-related sales and services and diversified into a range of related businesses. It was a trusted company all over the country, particularly in the South, and sales were assured to us. Soon after this, South India Corporation also approved our product to be supplied through their channels.

After South, I began addressing the Maharashtra and Gujarat markets, leaving UP for the time being because it was not developed. I also made many trips to Calcutta to appoint an agent and to look for direct customers.

Over a period of time, I was able to develop the gun factory at Jabalpur, where the Shaktiman truck is manufactured, as one of our biggest customers. To become approved suppliers for their enormous quantities, we had to register ourselves and follow the regular tender process. I must have made thirty or maybe even forty trips to Jabalpur for this purpose. At that time, Jabalpur was a tiny town and had nothing but the gun factory although it is now a significant tourist and trading centre.

After many visits to Jamshedpur, which I would visit via Calcutta or Patna, TELCO (now Tata Motors) also began sourcing their auto cable requirement from us. I visited their factory often and was interested to observe their production of the truck wiring harness which was assembled by women who worked in groups to lay the wire. Our importance as a vendor grew and soon they were relying on us for twenty percent of their auto-cable requirements. By the mid-1970s, this figure had risen to seventy percent. By this time, we had also established ourselves with Mahindra & Mahindra in Mumbai, Ashok Leyland in Chennai, and other large automobile manufacturers. Years later, Ashok Leyland was acquired by the Hindujas, with whom I have a close family relationship.

At the time when I was laying the Finolex dealer network, my objective was to have a large number of representatives. I would always select several small distributors in favour of a single one. I appointed each one of these distributors myself, evaluating them on various criteria. In the end, my decision would be based on a gut feeling. The answer "yes" or "no" would come to me very clearly, as if from an outside source. I can't say that I made no mistakes, but the business continued to grow at a reassuring pace.

When I think about how I had learnt to do all these things, I can only say that it was by observing others.

During this period, my reading and writing skills improved. It was now that my skills of management also began to develop. My basics of finance had been laid while working in the retail stores and with the moneylenders. I knew that by keeping all dealings straightforward, I would always have a spotless track record to show and this would favour future transactions.

I had learnt persistence and how to handle rejection. I knew that every dealer I appointed would speak to me in sweet tones and tell stories of all kinds with only one motive in mind; to get a higher commission from me and a higher profit for himself. Knowing this in advance, I would be prepared. I learnt to speak to them in their own language.

I had learnt strong systems and procedures while working with the armed forces. I had understood the importance of punctuality and the reputation for reliability that this simple habit could bring. Their quality standards were of the highest. I had also acquired an understanding of how the government offices function. I had learnt how to write different types of letters and become familiar with various types of documentation.

The most important quality which I built in myself during this phase was the discipline of commitment. Our biggest problem during this time was supply of raw material. When our authorized supply suddenly dried up and we had to buy from the open market, we never let our product quality suffer nor would we rush back to the customer asking for more than the quoted price. We preferred to absorb the rejection ourselves and suffer the losses rather than passing them on to the customers.

Buying raw material from the open market also raised our costs, and as a strategy we absorbed that cost also rather than letting it impact the customer's buying price. It was equally important that we delivered perfectly on schedule.

Sometimes it would happen that we would look at other products and notice that, for instance, our packaging quality was inferior. Without a second thought, we would improve the packaging we used. We made our time estimates carefully and ensured that we followed the schedules we had committed to. All these habits were being learnt for the first time. We tried them out and found that they brought us good working results as well as respect from those we dealt with. Over a period, they became as natural as breathing, our own personal qualities for all time.

It had been my habit from my earliest working memory, to note down all the learning in my diary when I returned home at the end of each day. I would list all the points that needed action. Every time an idea occurred to me, I would immediately note it down. It is my firm belief that ideas must be captured in an action list. I've always made a habit of carrying a small pocket diary to note reminders and small creative ideas as they occur to me which, if not recorded immediately, would be lost forever.

For me personally, growth was the most important thing. I would keep a close watch on the figures. How much product sale has taken place? How much stock do we have? I made sure I kept track of these things daily, weekly and monthly.

At this time we still had three lines of business-the retail shop Ramchand Bhagwandas & Co., our Defence contracts and our manufacturing company Indian Cable Industries. Since all the money was still accumulating in one repository, it was extremely important for me to keep a distinct focus on each separate revenue stream. I had to make decisions on which area I wanted to spend my time and energy and I knew that manufacturing was most exciting to me and most profitable in the long run. A trader feels satisfied reviewing how much he has made at the end of the day. But a manufacturer will wait for the end of the year to carry out the same exercise. Though I had no education or solid base of knowledge, instinct told me that this was the right path for me.

When one is in a situation like this, running a business with separate revenue streams, it is essential to clearly understand different profitability, potential, problems, resources required for each one separately, and how to make decisions within each business independently. When at the end of the month I would look at the bottom-line figure, my satisfaction would last only a few seconds before it became transformed into the question of how to make it a higher figure the following month, and that question would immediately be replaced by a series of actions that I must undertake to make it happen. I had to somehow raise my licence quota, procure more raw material, produce more, and sell more. I was completely driven by the idea of growth and nothing else, whether I was in Poona, Bombay, South India or Delhi. With no secretary to remind me of what I had to do, I scheduled my regular trips to various parts of the country, meetings and deadlines myself.

At this time I also realised that if we wanted to really grow, this Karve Road factory with its 2500 square foot area was not the place. I started looking for land, and by the middle of 1960 selected a stretch of five acres at Pimpri which was available at the rate of Rs. 9000 per acre.

My elder brothers disapproved spending so much money to move all the way across town to Pimpri, which was then something of a wild and remote jungle. If we had to spend so much money, they felt that one acre at Karve Road, at the going rate of Rs. 40,000 per acre, would be a much better choice.

It's true enough that at that moment we did not need more than a quarter acre for the operations that we were currently running. But unlike them, I was looking at large-scale expansion. In the end, I bought the five acres on my own. Fortunately, Kishan had full faith in my decision. He felt the same excitement and commitment towards our growing enterprise.

Just a few months later, when we received a huge order for cables from All India Radio, my decision was vindicated and my elder brothers agreed that we should go ahead and construct our factory at Pimpri with larger machinery, and space for assembling, packing and supplying as well as for administrative, finance and other support functions.

The Indian Government had decided that All India Radio (AIR) should be heard all over the country and they placed the cable order with us through the Delhi DGS&D. It was a prestigious order and another major landmark for us.

With great difficulty we procured sanction and started constructing our factory at Pimpri. By early 1961 we moved our operations along with all our equipment out of Karve Road.

To complete the AIR order on time, it was of utmost importance for us to procure raw material on time. Once again, I had to run around to the government offices, following the Poona-Bombay-Delhi-Bombay-Poona route as before.

When I think back about the way things turned out, I feel a strong sense of having been moved by destiny. Many people work hard, many follow similar principles of thorough integrity, focused goal orientation, and the highest commitment to quality. There has been nothing special about me. I have been extremely fortunate in the people I met, the team that joined my efforts and the circumstances that came my way. Right through my life an unseen force has guided my thoughts and actions and I can only attribute what little success I have achieved to that force.

4

A FINE STRETCH OF LAND

"Young people today should realise that the best form of learning and exposure is travel – planned travel, with a defined purpose. No matter how skilled, intelligent or educated you may be, it is only extensive travel and interaction with a wide range of people that will give you the experience, and the polish you need to be truly successful."

On the 12th of July 1961, civic disaster struck Poona when heavy rains caused the Panshet Dam to collapse.

Situated about 30 km from the main area of Pune, the Panshet area today is popular as a venue for picnics, with a long scenic drive out of the city. In those days it was nothing but jungle, blessed with large and extremely picturesque bodies of water.

These lakes had been providing the city's water supply right since historic times of Peshwa Rule in Pune. In the mid 1880s, the British dammed the Mutha river at Khadakvasla and some years after Independence, the Indian government built a series of dams upstream.

Just one year after the Panshet dam had begun being used to store water, unusually heavy rainfall struck the area. The normally calm and sluggish Mutha went into a spate, Heavy rain lashed down incessantly. My daughter Aruna and Kishan's son Vijay were babies hardly two years old, but they both still remember being taken to the Lakdi Pul in the city during intervals between heavy showers, to marvel at the rising water. After some days of this, the dam burst.

Huge columns of water flowed towards the city through the Mutha canals, submerging vast areas along the way, overtopping bridges, destroying homes and temples, and washing away people's belongings.

By the time the water receded it left behind massive debris and rotting grain. All basic amenities like the water supply, electricity and drainage were disrupted and took several days to be restored.

The Poona flood marked a major change in the history of the city. Several areas had been wiped out and people had fled the localities where their families had lived for centuries together. Even after the waters receeded, young people refused to go back to the wadas in the crowded city area. That was when places along the Satara Road and around Kothrud, which had been previously uninhabited, gradually developed with housing colonies.

It was after the flood that people started looking at Pimpri as a possible place of opportunity. There were very few industries at Pimpri then, mostly small units supplying to the Kirloskars who had been well established in Poona for decades. We had already moved there on the urging and encouraged by my friend Vasantrao Somwanshi, we had moved to our new premises in Pimpri. The first large companies at Pimpri were Hindustan Antibiotics and Ruston Hornby. Mahindra & Mahindra, Telco, Bajaj and the other giants there corporate giants today, only came later.

Naturally, the flood had a major impact on our lives as well. I was at the factory that day, when my wife phoned to tell me that our house had gone under water and the level was still rising.

By this time, we had bought ourselves a car, one of the old Morris Minors, and I drove back home. Kishan and I were now living at Prabhat Road Galli No. 4. The entire area was submerged. We saw our whole family standing on a raised surface with the children Aruna and Vijay in their arms, looking out at the four or five feet of water flooding over the area where our home lay now receding gradually. We spent the night in a small room at the factory in Pimpri.

Next day onwards, we began a massive cleaning-up operation. Many of our belongings were ruined. Much of it, such as our wedding photos and a lot of finery was irreplaceable.

Kishan and I were deeply immersed in our work, and not much involved in bringing the house back to order, which was taken care of by the women in the family. The most significant effect the flood had on me was a huge feeling of relief that we had been spared. Our imported machine and most of our equipment had already been shifted out of our Karve Road premises to the Pimpri location just in time. If this had not happened, it would have all been ruined and we would have had to start all over again, right from scratch. It would have been extremely difficult because by this time, the import of this type of machinery was completely banned. I wonder what would have happened? Our story would have been different, that is for sure. It is nothing but providence that kept us on this road.

Needless to say, the concept of insurance was unknown to us. The decision to move to Pimpri had been mine, against initial opposition and grumbles from my elder brothers. My pure belief that there was a driving force helping me to take decisions reinforced itself.

Till today, I firmly believe that when you are totally immersed in something, continuously taking feedback from the results of your actions and improvising based on that feedback to achieve better results, the right decisions come to you almost automatically.

By the late fifties, my days of ticketless travel were behind me, and I was now the proud owner of a First Class monthly pass on the Deccan Queen. Here the environment was quite different from what I had experienced on the milkman's train! People were well dressed and spoke in cultured tones, as befitted this historic passenger train connecting Bombay and Poona! It had a warm and cordial environment, and I made many friends with whom I have continued to remain in touch over the decades that followed. We talked to each other about the work we were doing. Besides businessmen like myself, I was also privileged to meet scientists, educationists, government officers, and ministers.

One of the most interesting people I met during this time, who was to become one of the major influences and guiding forces in my life, was Mr. A.R. Bhat. We were introduced to each other on the Deccan Queen, and got on well immediately. He was interested when he heard about the work I was doing, and for me, with the kind of help and guidance that he provided, he was like an angel sent from above.

Atmaram Raoji Bhat was one of those rare people of our time who worked tirelessly to change the destiny of our country. A brilliant student, he was a profound thinker, a public worker, and a practical economist. He had been active in the freedom movement, and in 1941 he set up the Indian Languages Newspaper Association.

Mr. Bhat firmly believed that the development of our nation could only come through the small-scale sector which, he felt, would generate employment and transform the economy in many ways as small industries had done in Japan. He never ceased his crusade against the government's belief that small scale would only give small value, and constantly found new ways to convince all whom he could that the SSIs would bring not just productivity but labour employment and general prosperity.

Despite not being connected with any industry or commercial establishment, he founded the MCCI in Poona in 1934, with the primary objective of promoting industries and in particular the small-scale sector. Looking at the development in cities like Pune, Ahmednagar, Kolhapur, Nasik, Satara, Sangli, Aurangabad, Jalgaon and others today tells how successful A.R. Bhat was in his mission. I joined the MCCI at his urging, and rarely missed a meeting over the years. I was benefited by this body in many different ways, and many years later, in 1992, I became President of this prestigious organization for two years. In 1998, agriculture was added to the scope of the Chamber's activities and it became the MCCIA.

Through the Chamber, A.R. Bhat was able to sponsor and promote Bank of Maharashtra, the Koyna Hydro Electric Project and various small industrialists in and around Poona, including me.

A. R. Bhat : 1905 - 1983   Courtesy : MCCIA

When I met him in the early 1960s, Mr. Bhat was a prominent figure and a member of the Bombay Legislative Council. He had made major contributions in various areas related to industrial development such as finance, taxation, planning, electricity and transport.

Despite his stature and high-level connections, he was one the most sincere and modest persons I had met. I was very privileged that he took personal interest in my case. He would help me with my applications to the government, accompanying me not just to Bombay in the Deccan Queen but on many occasions all the way to Delhi. Many times I would rush to his house with a problem, and he would quickly dictate a letter to his secretary, sign it and give it to me within a few minutes. Whenever he came with me to meet the Bombay Industry Commissioner, we would travel together on the Deccan Queen but he always bought his own ticket and would rather treat me to breakfast than let me spend a single paisa on him. He was a rare and wonderful human being and the kind of help he gave me was unique.

At home too, many changes had taken place.

My mother had been pressing me to get married and settle down for a long time. I was already 28 years old and Kishan, or K.P. as we now referred to him, was also of marriageable age. She was keen that we should have someone to take care of us since she felt she was getting older.

When I finally agreed to settle down, it happened that our mother found a match for both Kishan and me at the same time and our marriages were fixed for the same day, the thirteenth of December 1958. They were both traditionally arranged rishtas. We had met briefly in a small restaurant, in the presence of some relatives. When I saw Mohini, there was no hesitation. The "yes" came to me without a thought.

Both girls were from Shikarpuri families. Mohini was the daughter of Bhojraj and Shantidevi Menda. Her family had settled in Bombay after partition. Kishan's in-laws had settled in Madras. We got married in Bombay, returned to Poona the next day and went right back to work.

Bombay, 13ᵗʰ December 1958: Pralhad weds Mohini

I was right in the middle of supplying a large Defence order and there were a great many activities pending. When I think back today, I realise that my marriage was a very simple ceremony, without much enthusiasm or fanfare, just a routine necessity that had to be gone through. Surely if our father had been alive, things would have been different, and there would have been a proper festive wedding environment. Though there was now enough income coming in from Defence contracts as well as from the retail shop, there was no excitement of shopping, or getting jewellery made, sending invitations, making arrangements for guests, hiring musicians or any of the other activities normally associated with traditional Indian weddings. Nobody in the family suggested that we should go away together on holiday for a few days. We were just given a shoddy room to spend our wedding night. The important new members entered our family without the joy, caring or gifts of love that they deserved.

At many times in my life as I grew older, I missed the comfort and protection of having a father. It was naturally never as intense as it had been in early childhood. Over the years, my experience taught me that joint families work much better when parents have power and provide a central driving force to the unit. My mother was a subdued and low-key person and had lost her sense of authority many years ago. I was so immersed in my work that my family life, though an important necessity, was not a priority to focus on. It was many years before my wife and I enjoyed our first holiday together.

After marriage, home became a place of comfort and warmth, with someone to talk to and to care for me. For both Kishan and me, work was our full-time priority. He would be at the factory until late, and I would be travelling all the time. Yet it was always a pleasant feeling when I was away to know that there was someone who cared for me at home. Fortunately, Mohini was very understanding and gave me her complete support. She realised that my work was the most important thing in my life and she understood that for me to be a successful businessman, long hours and endless efforts were essential. She participated in my struggle without a second thought or single complaint.

Bombay, 13th December 1958: Kishan weds Sunita

Our daughter Aruna was born in 1959 at Dr. Y.V. Pathak's nursing home on Tilak Road. I was away at the time, perhaps in Delhi or in South India and came home to be with my family. It was a good feeling to look at her and feel that this is my child! However, I was so engrossed in my work that I was unable to spend much time there and was on the road again in three or four days. By the time our son Prakash was born in 1963, we were already well established at Pimpri and had successfully completed the All India Radio order.

My work now involved so much travelling that I would be away from home for thirty or even forty days at a time. Communication was limited and expensive and it was difficult to keep in touch while travelling. To speak to someone in another city, you had to dial the telephone operator and book a "trunk" or long-distance call, then wait for several hours for it to come through. Naturally this was not possible while one was travelling. So my family would not know I was coming home until they actually saw me arrive.

All this travelling gave me a lot of experience in dealing with different types of people. With everyone I met, whether a shopkeeper, or a dealer who stocked our cables or different manufacturers, who were our competitors or employees of other companies – there would be some learning, some opportunity to expand my skills and knowledge. Young people today should realise that the best form of learning and exposure is travel – planned travel, with a defined purpose. No matter how skilled, intelligent or educated you may be, it is only extensive travel and interaction with a wide range of people that will give you the experience, and the polish you need to be truly successful.

Sometimes, for months at a stretch I would travel daily from Poona to Bombay, leaving at the crack of dawn and reaching home late at night, only to start again early next morning. Though my in-laws lived in Bombay and I got along very well with Mohini's brothers Gopaldas, Ghanshamdas, Ramesh and Mahesh, I could very rarely spare the time to visit them. However, on the occasions when my work was incomplete at the end of the day, I could spend the night at their home if I wished.

All the while that I was away, Mohini would answer phone calls and take messages for the business, which she would write down and send to the factory. Many of these phone calls were phonograms regarding our Defence contracts. In those days the procedure was for telegram messages to first be delivered as phonograms, which were read out by operators over the telephone. There were times when we received ten or even twenty telegrams in a day! These calls came at all hours, right through the day or night. Most of them were several pages long and contained tedious, elaborate details containing code numbers, technical specifications, quantities required, expected date of delivery and all the other highly important order information.

The telegraph office would phone and someone would read out all this, and Mohini would write it all down patiently and carefully in the diary she kept next to the telephone for this purpose.

Since I was away for long stretches at a time, I was not even aware of the kind of inconvenience Mohini faced, but when it came to my notice I took special permission from the General Post Office to stop making the phone calls and the telegrams then began to be delivered to us during the day.

Even after that, while I was at home, the phone played an important though disruptive part in our lives. My distributors from all over the country would have to place trunk calls to give me their orders. Once office hours began, people all over the country would be trying to get in touch with one another, and the trunk lines would be completely jammed. To avoid this rush, my important customers from Madras and Ernakulam and all the other places would call me as soon as they awoke, sometimes as early as 5 a.m. The maximum number of phone calls would be before 7 in the morning. At Pimpri, till as late as some time in 1963, we shared Vasantrao Somvanshi's phone line. Vasantrao was one of my dear friends. He had been president of the MCCI, which was how I had met him. He was very well-connected and helped me in many ways. Seeing my struggle and hectic lifestyle, he often invited me home to join him for lunch during the workday. He had been allotted a phone because his home was in the same plot and when he saw the kind of struggle we were having with our communications, he kindly laid down a parallel telephone line for us. We now had a telephone in our office. His office would answer the phone, and if the call turned out to be for us, someone would crank a device with a long handle attached to their instrument, winding it until someone in our office picked up the phone.

Within a few weeks it had become clear that the phone calls we were receiving far outnumbered his. Our cable work had started in earnest and distributors from all over the country, as well as our suppliers from Bombay were calling non-stop. Exhausted by the constant cranking of the long handle, Vasantrao quietly transferred his line to us and kept the parallel line for his own calls. The word "dialling" actually comes from the old dials we had, large, round and rather stiff; quite unlike today's press-button numbers and speed dialling. They were well known to break the nails of telephone operators and in extreme cases even give them calluses on their dialling fingers. For the past few years it had become my responsibility to sort the morning tapal or mail, marking each correspondence to the one of us who could best deal with it. There would be tenders, orders, references for purchase and so on. I maintained a mail log with these details for further reference and follow-up. It was my habit to write the initials of the person it was to be sent to, and this practice of referring to my brothers by their initials rather than their full names took root. Soon we had become known as B.P., R.P., P.P., and K.P.

I had begun to feel the need for more space and a better standard of living and we had rented the ground floor of a house at Prabhat Road Galli No. 4. My eldest brother B.P. had moved into a rented flat on Fergusson College Road. Ramchand, or R.P., lived in a flat opposite the Kamla Nehru Park, as he now preferred Poona to Bombay. We had hired a manager to look after the Bombay end of our business which R.P. had been doing till then.

As we earned more, all the money was spent on expansion of our business. At home, we continued to be very conservative in our spending. Our commitment was to build and grow. We were very conscious of our bank liabilities and the fact that because the company was growing, our profits did not really belong to us.

When we finally bought a car, it was more because we needed to travel than for the luxury or status of having a car. For a long time, we used the factory vehicle, a multi-purpose three-wheeled delivery van. We would sit next to the driver, or travel in the box with the goods. Coming home from Pimpri, it was pitch dark at night, but in the morning it was a pleasant drive with fields lining both sides of the road.

Poona, 1966: Deepak, Aruna, Prakash, Vijay

I was so busy that I never had much time to spend with my children. We went on family outings occasionally, but I never visited their school. These days fathers are much more involved, which I think is a very good thing. I have only one regret in my life and that is that I did not give more of my time and attention to my wife, my children and my mother. I was working at such a tempo that it just never struck me that I had a commitment and responsibility to them as well. I would get up in the morning and race to work, coming home only late at night. I consider myself extremely fortunate that despite this I had the maximum possible support from my wife and children.

Today I spend as much time with my grandchildren as I can, and advise my children to give them their full time and attention especially while they are still young. Once a child finishes school and reaches the age of sixteen, other influences become much more important than parents. That's why it is essential for us to devote every possible effort to spending time with children and passing on the family links and traditions at a young age. If possible, spend time with them as you expose them to different creative and sporting pursuits. Let them choose pursuits of their own inclination. Every child is different, so do not attempt to club siblings to learn the same things at the same pace. If you never have time to talk and listen to them, you would have lost the only small avenue of influence that parents can have on their children. Even when your children take more cues from their friends than from you, never forget that they need your guidance and have the right to ask for it as long as they live. Always be prepared to give the best guidance and advice. They deserve it.

I remember a few precious occasions when my son was a baby, taking him in a buggy to the Kamala Nehru park along with my wife and daughter. By this time, K.P. also had another son, Deepak, born in 1962. Their family lived nearby and on the rare days when the two of us came home early from work, we would meet in the evenings and the children would play together. Our families have always been very close. Mohini and K.P.'s wife Sunita got along extremely well and shared the household chores, preparing lunch boxes for the children, ironing their uniforms and taking them to school. They often baby-sat for each other. The children were all close in age and they enjoyed each other's company very much.

1968, Pune : P. P. and Mohini Chhabria

During the period from 1956 till around 1975, though I was travelling for long stretches of time, whenever I was in Poona, I tended to spend almost every evening in the company of our Chartered Accountant Mr. Balasaheb Bhide, seeing to my taxation and accounting matters after an early dinner. Mr. Bhide was a partner in the firm appointed to audit our accounts. As the person responsible for my business and answerable to my various stakeholders, it was extremely important for me to understand every aspect of these essentials. He always made time to see me after office hours. Working along with him I learnt how to read and oversee the maintenance of accounts. His training helped me give my company an excellent foundation right from the beginning and we have always maintained the standards that he laid for us. Mr. Bhide was one of the most important teachers and I remember him often with gratitude and affection. We spent so much time together that Mohini and his wife Malatitai also became good friends.

The years of most intense growth and change in lifestyle occurred soon after we moved to Pimpri. Between 1961 and 1966, all four brothers had bought a car each. We were now staying separately and separate transport was a necessity, not a luxury. B.P. and R.P. were managing the shop and had full control. K.P. and I were in charge of the factory. We each had equal shares of each and equal profits, but the two businesses were managed separately. I still remember the day in 1966 when B.P., my eldest brother, paid a visit to me at Pimpri. He wanted some of his share of money, because he had seen a bungalow he liked and decided to buy it for himself. I did not hesitate for even a second. I knew immediately that this was a very good idea. It was time for each of us to buy property.

K.P. and I bought a 34,000 square foot plot at the Model Colony and divided it in two. K.P. built a house for himself there in 1973 and continues to live there. B.P. moved into the bungalow he had wanted to. I was living in a rented place, Vimal Sadan, on Prabhat Road, Galli No. 11. Our landlord here was G. K. Patil and our families got along very well, though my children initially missed our previous home. There we had been tenants of Mr. Hanchate and my children had been fond of his wife Malati, who cooked up many delicious treats for them. B. J. Rathi and his family lived across the road and we had become very close friends. B. J. Rathi was later a valuable member of the Finolex board, right untill his sad demise in March 2007.

Vimal Sadan, 1974

I was somewhat settled now, and once again made time for my favourite pastime of music. A sitar was presented to me, and both Mohini and I began to take lessons. During this period, I had become more conscious of my place in society. My success in business had earned me a certain amount of recognition. Though I was never interested in attending parties or late nights, as a businessman I saw the need to have a circle of well-placed acquaintances. Every person who has something to sell knows the importance of being a member of a wealthy, influential circle; having access to people who can buy or can connect you with those who will buy.

I became a member of the Rotary Club which had their weekly meetings every Monday evening at the Poona Club. This gave me some exposure to Poona society. I soon also joined the Poona Club, paying the enviable sum of Rs. 500 for life membership. I took my children to the club on Saturdays when I was at home. It was a special treat for them and we would sometimes watch a movie there in the evenings.

However, I never got into the habit of playing cards. It is still something I do not know how to do. I've never been to the races. I do have time for these pursuits these days, but I'm least interested. Though there were many who pursue these things, I never had the inclination and have been busy and content doing what I really want to do. It's not that one way is bad and the other is good. Each one of us have to decide how we want to spend our time. Kishan and me were just too immersed in our work.

At Mr. Bhat's insistence, I had joined the MCCI and it added value to my aspirations in many ways. I attended all the meetings and received many useful inputs. After the meetings I would sometimes meet the speaker of the day and discuss important matters such as labour relations, machinery, raw material, and so on. Some would give me books to read or instruct me on new concepts.

In 1968, we were introduced by one of our acquaintances to another extremely helpful person who taught us one of the most essential aspects of manufacturing. This was Dr. Sundari Vaswani, and through her efforts we were able to set up a successful statistical and costing department. Dr. Vaswani was a consulting advisor with the Kirloskar group companies,

MICCI, 1960: P. P. Chhabria(no. 1), S. L. Kirloskar(no. 3), Damanna Potdar (no. 4), A. R. Bhat (no. 8), and others.

travelling from Bombay to spend a day at each factory at regular intervals. We requested her to provide us with her consultancy as well.

Dr. Vaswani was a committed and dynamic person, full of enthusiasm in her area of expertise. She added tremendous value to our organization for a very low fee, and also inspired our team to participate in the process of data collection, training and motivating them to fill the forms she had designed. She was very friendly with them, spending the whole day at our factory and eating lunch with the workers.

Dr. Vaswani was a very fine lady who added great value to our enterprise, helping us to use statistical data to identify our weaknesses. She continued helping us even after she moved to Delhi in 1988. She was the sister of Dada J.P. Vaswani, and niece of the revered Sadhu Vaswani, though not an active member of the mission.

I have the MCCI to thank for my first interaction with foreigners as well. My English was still not very fluent but when the Chamber invited professors and industrialists from various countries specifically to visit us and train our entrepreneurs, Kishan and I made it a point to bring them to our factory. We had machines from Japan, Germany, and the U. S., and visitors from these countries were particularly happy to share their knowledge with us. Over a period, we learnt the basics of setting up a well-managed production unit with separate departments for the stores activity with raw material and finished goods, for purchase, accounting, and other activities. We learnt to organize and set up our systems so well that they would grow with us as our organization grew.

With the earning from the All India Radio order, we began to invest in more machinery. Kishan managed the production. He had built up a small but devoted workforce. They always stood by us and we never experienced production delays or labour unrest. At the Karve Road factory we had increased our labour force to around 25 and at Pimpri this number grew steadily and by the mid-1970s we had around 100.

I had been associated for a long time with manufacturing giants like TVS and this association benefited us in many ways. Their founder, T.V. Sundaram Iyengar, had four sons and they were well known for their simplicity, transparency and honourable way of doing business. TVS

Chennai, 1995: Receiving long - association award
from S. Narayanan of Madras Auto Service (TVS)

was using high-level corporate governance, and the strategy resulted in long-term shareholder value. At that time, however, it was just the actions of a decent man with his customers' best interests at heart. I was privileged to witness and learn from their business philosophy and mature HR practices.

Following their example of strong focus on benefit to workers, we introduced the government's Employee State Insurance and Provident Fund benefit for workers even before we had registered ourselves as an SSI. We initiated worker cooperative societies where each worker would contribute a small monthly amount, and a corpus was built up so that when anyone needed money, for medical treatment or education or any other reason, they could approach the cooperative society for a loan. Today it has reached the tune of a few crores of rupees. The corpus is run by a committee that changes every five years and has helped many of our workers.

We also implemented simple schemes such as providing a twice-daily tea service long before this became a practice in every organization, leading to a feeling among the labour that we cared for their comfort.

Our factory was still a little isolated and we all had to carry our lunch boxes from home. However, again taking a cue from the TVS practices, we soon established a staff canteen. This became a full-fledged operation of its own, very well designed and efficiently serving a hot and nutritious meal at a subsidised rate of just Re 1 to each person. We began offering systematised leave privileges, something that only large multinational or government companies then offered.

Our land was conveniently located so that workers could walk to work from the Pimpri station. Factories at that time had a system that if the worker was late by more than fifteen minutes, a half day's wage would be deducted from his pay packet. Now Kishan knew very well that the train was frequently late. He did not expect his people to jump out and run to the factory to be on time, and made sure that on occasions when this happened, the worker was not penalised. It was just a question of understanding the situation and making simple adjustments to accommodate it. This gave them the clear message that we were reasonable and cared for them, and they reciprocated wholeheartedly.

Pimpri, 1963 : Yashwantrao Chavan & Morarji Desai with
Finolex Family
1st row: K. P. (no.1), Chavan (no.2), Morarjibhai (no.3), R. P. (no.5), U. S. Anikhandi (no.8)3rd row: N. P. (no.2)

Pimpri, 1963: D. V. Potdar, Morarji Desai, K. P. Chhabria

However, we were still a small-scale industry. Though our workforce had increased, we were still unable to attract qualified engineers to work with us. K.P. was still working with simple matriculates or even completely uneducated workers, training them to use our sophisticated machinery.

Similarly, senior managers were reluctant to join us, preferring to first apply to the other large factories now established at Pimpri. Working with those who did join, I trained them in accounts, purchase, marketing, correspondence, document preparation, filing, follow-up and all the other useful skills I myself had learnt from others while on the job.

In 1963, our factory was one of the only small-scale industries in Pimpri, and we were honoured by a visit from Yashwantrao Chavan, Chief Minister of Maharashtra, along with Morarji Desai, then Finance Minister of the country. Even at this late stage and with all my success in business, I was not very politically aware and only knew that Morarji Desai was a very firm, disciplined leader, transparent, clean, and idealistic, who took quick decisions. I felt convinced that he would help us in our initiative.

At this time, I had also begun to buy up adjoining land with the personal savings Mohini and I had made.

Though we had not occupied much of our five acres, having built up just a quarter acre or so, I would often gaze out at the farming land around me, knowing that we could expand over all this area.

When I spoke to Mohini, she said she had saved Rs. 10,000. I felt that this was a big achievement. We lived a simple life in a rented flat and she never complained or craved for more. Instead, she had been regularly setting aside small sums of money and she now offered it to me to reserve an additional five acres, suggesting that we then pay the rest of the money in instalments.

I spoke to the owners, and they agreed. I bought an additional five acres in the name of Indian Cable Industries without my elder brothers' knowledge. By mid-1966, I was in possession of twenty-five acres.

Pimpri, 1968: Prakash and P. P. Chhabria at the
Finolex Dussehra Pooja

One day we had a visit from the Industry Commissioner, the IAS officer Mr. N.W. Desai, asking us to surrender nine acres of this land. He said that this was required for industrial development. The Industry Commissioner was not satisfied that Finolex would make use of this land whereas a neighbouring industrialist, he said, required it for immediate use. There was huge pressure on me. They asked why I was buying land when I had no money in my pockets and insisted that I surrender it immediately.

I was stunned at this gross injustice. I had no personal contacts at high levels or any other resource by which I could countermand this decision. I had no choice but to comply, which I did with bitter feelings. The record of this transaction is available with the MCCIA as well as with the relevant government bodies. I was now left with sixteen acres, but was later able to add one acre to the property.

Some years later Mr. Desai became head of the Bombay Municipal Corporation. We had maintained contact all this while. He now apologized to me, explaining that he had been under tremendous political pressure and had no choice but to extort the land from me. He offered to help me acquire land anywhere in the state. I declined.

Many other small-scale industrialists faced similar situations. The only consolation we had was that when they snatched away our lands or other prized assets they would grant us a higher quota of raw material by which our business could increase.

At this time, Finolex was one of the many unknown companies. There were many others producing cables, some joint venture companies with the British: Fort Gloucester, Cable Corporation of India (CCI), Nicco Universal, Asian Cables, Devidayal Cable Industries, Incab, Asian RPG, Oriental, Delton and even public- sector companies like Hindustan Cables. Of the top twenty cable companies, Finolex was a poor twentieth. Over the next few years, however, we were to establish and consolidate ourselves as one of the most powerful brands in this country.

From 1962 onwards we began building the brand, working first with Ganesh Tambe who ran the Poona advertising agency Tom & Bay, and as our needs increased, moving to a company called Adverds, run by a

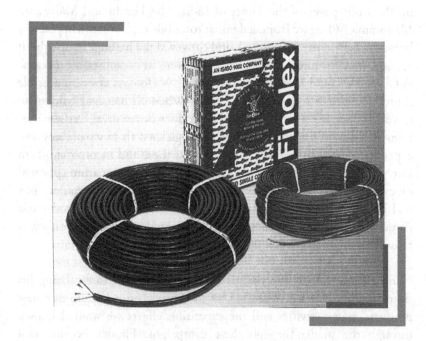

Parsi gentleman Baji Nariman Maloo, in Bombay. I spent days together with Nariman, and learnt from him the basics of Public Relations and Advertising.

The colours and basic designs chosen by Nariman for Finolex visiting cards, letterheads, product boxes and so on worked so well right from the start that till today we have never found a reason to change them. He designed a kit for me to carry as I travelled all over the country, visiting shop after shop to appoint distributors. This was later used by all the salesmen of Finolex. Besides brochures, price lists and actual product samples, he also included a sample card. This he designed with a piece of auto cable stuck on the card and the illustration and text was of such high international quality, that it helped my clients overcome any reservations they might have had in switching from imported to an Indian product.

Through this process I began to understand advertising aesthetics and the consumer mindset. Nariman's work continues to be associated with our brand. It was Nariman who planned the highly successful Finolex ad campaigns. As early as 1964, Finolex had quarter-page advertisements on the front pages of the Times of India, The Hindu and Malayalam Manorama. When we launched our automobile cable, Nariman placed a horse carriage in the foreground, and conveyed the message that without a good quality automobile cable, you were very vulnerable because your vehicle could break down anywhere! We looked at every possible source for ideas to promote the brand. When Kishan and I began to travel abroad, we would bring back product boxes or advertisements. I would always take notes of ideas I had gleaned from what I saw and experienced. Nariman and I would discuss these and incorporate them into our advertisements. For some years, Nariman's signature appeared on every box of Finolex cables as it had come to our notice that our box had been duplicated, and spurious cables were being sold under our name! For a long time, having his signature on the box was the only way to differentiate the genuine Finolex boxes.

Nariman also taught me the art of sending press releases. Using his simple techniques we were able to effectively communicate our new products, new activities and the expansion efforts we wanted known through the media. Through these campaigns, Finolex became well known in all the major cities and every centre where the market for cables

1970: P. P. and K. P. receive award from
Chadrakant Kirloskar for optimum use of generator

was strong. Initially concentrating in Bombay and then the South, we moved towards the North and then East after some years, establishing for ourselves a solid customer mindshare that would stand us in good stead in the years to come.

As our business grew, I often had the opportunity to get personal publicity for myself, but I always stepped away from the public glare. I only looked for publicity for my company, never for myself.

Today we have a variety of cables, but even by the early 1970s we were already supplying large quantities of single-core and multi-core cables, auto and battery cables, winding wires, flat cables, coaxial cables, and more, to the government and industry through our network of distributors.

By 1970, we were running three shifts at the factory. Ours was a continuous process plant and to maximise our asset value, K.P. had devised a system by which we were working seven days a week, 24 hours a day. As we used the same space and other resources, this was one simple way of reducing overheads. Very soon, other small factories in the area had begun following our example.

By now we had reconciled ourselves to buying raw material in the open market, while continuously trying to get our licence increased. Mr. A. R. Bhat continued to accompany me many times to Delhi during this period. In the 1950s, for an asset value of up to Rs. 10 lakhs, you were in the "small scale" sector. By the time we reached the magic figure, the bar had been moved up to Rs. 25 lakhs and it continued to be out of our reach.

Moving in this way, from nothing to small-scale to medium-scale and then finally, some years later, to large-scale, gave me a through grounding of minute functional experience of every level, and I am really grateful for this. There was a different and very specific type of learning from each phase. This is what gave me the training that made me capable of continuing to lead even as we grew.

Just as a painter will always visualise and paint and a singer will continuously listen to himself and practise to make his voice perfect, in the same way for an entrepreneur continuous growth is nothing but a simple necessity, something that you cannot survive without. We now began to recruit experienced people to take care of our accounts, procurement, and marketing. But it was still my job to supervise and control, and often to travel with them for support. While I was busy strategising and travelling, K.P. planned and laid down quality standards, and enhanced our plant capacity by bringing in new machinery and installing it through our different phases of expansion. He continued experimenting with samples of different types. I would bring home samples of every new product I came across, and he would examine and work to replicate them with great enthusiasm. He also began travelling to exhibitions in Germany to learn the latest developments in the field. Distributors watched us with interest. Our continuous stream of lucrative new products made our company attractive to them.

It also continued to be my job to interact with our bankers to expand our credit facility. As before, I followed my principles of making payments and submitting the required periodic reports on time, and complete transparency of the flow of funds. We were still banking with the Central Bank of India. On one occasion some time around 1964, a new branch of a local bank offered to finance us at a lower rate of interest. This was an attractive proposition, and they promptly advanced us Rs. 85,000 towards machinery we were importing from Japan at the time. However, they stipulated that we close the Central Bank account and work exclusively with them. Without a second thought, we returned the Rs. 85,000. We closed our account with them and continued to bank with the Central Bank of India.

One of my key requirements in business was flexibility and I did not want to be in a position where my bankers could dictate terms to us. Nowadays with a centralised information system available on computer, it is easier for the bank to understand a company's credit history and credit rating. But at that time, it was quite common and reasonable for a bank to put this stricture. However, it was my decision to do my work without pressure inflicted in any way from my bankers. I consulted my friends and some of the senior businessmen I knew, and they also advised that I had made the right decision.

With all the restrictions we faced from the government, we businessmen were terrified of monopoly and the kind of pressure it could bring.

Of course I don't blame the bank for trying to make this kind of arrangement; for them it is just their business to protect the money of their shareholders with interest. In our case it was not practical for another reason; a local bank had limited branches whereas by now our business was spread all over India.

By this time we had a reasonably good flow of raw material. Our bankers had faith in us, and increasingly competent and committed people were joining our team. However, till around 1970, we kept striving to move into the medium-scale bracket.

I was travelling to Delhi every month, sometimes twice a month, trying to get a medium-scale licence. Every official I met would complain of the lack of raw material. I would often be chased away from outside the office. I would be waiting patiently outside and a peon would be sent to tell me, "Saab is busy, come next month." The market was controlled by a few big players with political clout who would share the raw material between themselves. They were against the small players because more players meant smaller share for each individually. Often, they were able to keep us out.

Even with the All India Radio order, where it was the government's duty to see that we got the raw material to complete it, we had been able to deliver on time only by buying material from the open market.

By now people had begun to appreciate the kind of quality we were giving them and our products were in great demand. We had a distributor network all over the country. Whatever we produced would enter the market immediately. There were always people waiting for our cables. The demand was more than the supply.

By around the end of 1970, I visited Iran on holiday with Mohini. This was our first holiday abroad, and a very important occasion indeed for us!

In those days, foreign travel was the privilege of only a very few elite Indians and we considered ourselves extremely fortunate indeed to be part of this society. The government had placed severe restriction on the amount of foreign exchange those travelling abroad were entitled

Bombay, 1970: Warm sean-off on the first holiday abroad

Gopaldas & Mani Menda, Sulochana & B. P., Parvatibai (P. P.'s mother), N. P., Jayshree, Mohini, P. P., Jyoti

to, which made it impossible to travel to another country with dignity. Also, because Indian manufacturing was still in its infancy, consumer products in this country were crude and rather backward. There was a feverish craze for foreign goods of any type which today is hard to envision. Radio broadcasts gave us news, but this was controlled by the government. Import of books and magazines into the country was restricted. To leave the country and step outside this fantasy world was a dream, and it was a great thing for us to be able to do it. I remember on a trip to Singapore, being fascinated to learn that you could get a formal suit tailored and ready to take home in less than 24 hours!

Two of Mohini's sisters, Lalita and Madhu, had married into the Hinduja family. The family's links with Iran went back to 1919, when P.D. Hinduja had come to that country at a very young age to seek his fortune. Starting with nothing, within a few years he had earned enough to set up a business that was to form the foundation of the Hinduja empire.

Lalita's husband Girdhar had died at an early age, and she had moved back to Bombay where her father-in-law had given her administrative charge of Hinduja Hospital. Madhu and her husband Srichand were also living in Bombay but Srichand was now our host in Iran.

Iran was a very beautiful country. In those days it was particularly lively and advanced, and still under the regime of Mohammad Reza Pahlavi, Shah of Iran. I had been stressed and overworked in the few weeks preceding the trip, and it was good to get away to this lovely place. We had a pleasant, relaxed holiday of eight or ten days there. Though it was a purely personal visit, I did look for opportunities to set up business in Iran since there were so many limitations in India. I did not find any such opportunities at that time, but by chance I met an industrialist, Baghubhai Patel, who was to give me my next big business growth opportunity.

When Mr. Patel heard about my business, he told me that he had a cable plant in Lonavala which he was keen to sell. I was very interested. When I went back to India, I made inquiries. There was no industrial belt in Lonavala. However, acquiring his company, Alfa Rubber Ltd., would give us two major advantages. One, it was a public limited company, though not listed on the stock exchange. Two, it had an industrial licence, higher even than medium scale which we had recently acquired. In addition to these, it had a fully mechanised plant which would greatly increase our output. Though the name said "rubber", it only manufactured PVC products.

I discussed the matter with K.P. and we decided to go ahead and buy Alfa Rubber. . He never questioned my decisions. If I gave him a paper and told him to sign it, he would do so without asking a single question. Though all five of us brothers were very close, our ideas about business were different. B.P. and R.P. were not particularly interested in our growing manufacturing activity and preferred to focus their time and attention trading at the shop, which was also doing extremely well.

Many families break up over business arguments and decisions. It is another of the blessings of my life that the bonds with my brothers were strong enough to overcome our disagreements at work. For a long time after we separated the businesses, we continued to be partners in each other's companies, but today our families run separate outfits. The shop Ramchand Bhagwandas & Co. is run by my eldest brother's two sons and continues to be a very successful trading entity. Ramchand's and Narayan's families are also in separate businesses of their own. The family members continue to own some shares in Finolex Cables and Finolex Industries. Our strength as a very close-knit family has flourished even though we chose to go separate ways in business.

Alfa Rubber had a fully imported plant with machinery larger and more powerful than Indian Cable Industries. This meant that we were now not only entitled to a much larger share of raw material from the government but also had the required processing machinery to scale up our production! We fixed a share price with Mr. Patel and bought hundred percent shares of Alfa Rubber, and decided that it must be merged with Indian Cable Industries. To do this, it was necessary for us to dissolve the partnership company, and create a new limited company. Naturally, none of us had any idea how to do this. We began to learn the significance of shareholders, stock, the board of directors, how corporate companies are run, the treasury department, shareholder department; a great deal of learning indeed! It was an exhilarating experience. I learnt that in any limited company the secretarial department is very important. We were lucky to have very good people on our team and we built a strong department which continues to function extremely well till even today and we have now established with strong corporate governance.

K.P. was fully involved in managing and implementing technology. The scope of my responsibilities now increased and there was a great deal of work including discussions and planning with our Chartered Accountants. Mr. Bhide rose to the challenge, and along with a brilliant company lawyer, Mr. V. N. Mysore who had tragically lost his eyesight some years previously and our Finance Controller & Company Secretary, Mr. M. Y. Paranjape who had joined us after several years with Bank of India, drafted all the necessary documents. Since we were all busy with various aspects of work during the day, we would meet at ten at night and work till midnight, a routine that continued for several months. By the end of 1972, all the paperwork was complete and we were ready to move forward. As the mover of the whole process, I had been named Chairman and Managing Director, and my three brothers, Directors. We also decided to merge the two plants, and move the plant machinery from Lonavala to Pimpri where we still had plenty of land to build new sheds. At this time, our major products were still the PVC auto cables, single-core, multi-core flexible, house wiring and general purpose cables. But with the heavy-duty machinery we now had, we were able to extend our range and start producing power cables and other heavy-duty cables.

I also invited other directors to join our board, knowing that this would give the company benefit of wider perspective and experience and also bring more business discipline, which is invariably a major issue in a family-run company as ours had been. One of the first outsiders to join our board was Mr. C.V. Jog who had been Chairman of Bank of Maharashtra. He was a fine individual and brought respect and value to our board.

By the end of 1973, we changed the name of the new company to Finolex Cables Ltd. This was a major transition for the company. The new name brought us respect in the market when advertising our product, and when corresponding with multinational companies or the government. While in Iran, I sensed good potential for export of our cables and we started doing so not just to that country Iran, but to other areas in the Middle East including Iraq. R. P. was made Director in charge of Exports.

Exports brought us added recognition from the government because it meant that we were bringing much-needed foreign exchange into the country. Raw material was easily sanctioned against export orders, which made the work easier and more profitable.

The years 1957 to 1967 had been spent in building up our industry, investing in new machinery and continuously expanding. From 1967 till around 1977, we focussed on giving more value to the company and our products. By the mid-1970s, Finolex had entered a new and much larger league, but our struggle was by no means over. We were now competing with large, established players and had to once again make the extra push required for new market entry. Around this time, the government had a new surprise in store for us and announced a range of restrictions on the use of copper in cables.

India has poor copper resources, but is rich with deposits of bauxite, the chief ore of aluminium. To popularize the use of aluminium, the government began to promote its use as a substitute for copper and raised the import duty on copper to a very high level, and in the late 1970s, introduced the Copper Control Order. Under this order, the use of copper was prohibited in a range of applications, including house wiring.

It was well known that aluminium was a suitable material for power cables and transmission lines, but not for use in household wiring or in industries. Aluminium is not malleable and wire made from it will break easily if twisted. It is also less conductive than copper. However, aluminium can be used for power cables, where these limitations are not pertinent.

The Bureau of Indian Standards (then the ISI) formulated specifications for cables made with aluminium conductor which were formerly applicable only to copper.

Another curb of the Copper Control Order was that copper was available only to registered cable manufacturers through the import licence allocated by the government. The manufacture of household electrical wiring was also restricted to small-scale manufacturers, who had a further advantage in terms of Excise Duty and Sales Tax.

Here we were, sitting proud with our industrial licence, finally ready to enter full-scale production of copper cables which was one of our main products, and we were now being told by the government that we could make only aluminium cables! How ironical that soon after leaving behind our small- scale status, which we had struggled for years on end to do, the small-scale sector was being given benefits and we ourselves were put to a disadvantage.

To circumvent this ruling and resume our cable manufacturing activity, K.P. now worked with his team of engineers to produce a household wire with a design that would enable us to begin manufacture despite all the strictures of the government.

At that time, the copper wire in popular use was either solid copper like 18 gauge, or with a three-wire construction. Various other sizes were also in use.

The Finolex team now devised special constructional details with more wires of smaller diameter bunched together to form the conductor. Using 14 copper wires of 0.3mm diameter, we produced the 1.0 sq mm size which was even more flexible than before. The other approved sizes, namely 1.5, 2.5, and 4.0 sq mm were also redesigned in a similar manner to produce a complete range of flexible wires which did not fall under the range of specifications forbidden by the Copper Control Order.

We advertised these wires by emphasizing their utility in concealed wiring, where they could be easily pulled through a conduit without any damage.

The new design was well accepted and was soon copied by our competitors. These were also approved by leading contractors and consultants and greatly liked by the consumers. Very soon it became established as the new industry standard. The Copper Control Order was finally withdrawn in 1991, after several petitions from various organizations requesting the Government to review and modify the order for the benefit of the public.

Copper has many advantages and it has taken more than a decade to undo the nationwide damage done by the Copper Control Order.

The Copper Control Order was not the only setback we faced in the 1970s. It was a time of recession, and I remember one meeting called by Mr. S.L. Kirloskar at the MCCI. He announced that the time had come for us to conserve resources. He advised us to make investment decisions very carefully and reduce costs at all levels. He suggested that we put a freeze on recruitment until the situation improved. The markets dipped and our growth floundered for a while. Though this brought our profits down, we were conservative spenders and our overheads were very low. None of us was relying on high salaries, and there was no heavy bank burden on the company balance sheet.

Sales dropped during this period, and my team and I travelled all over the country even to get small orders. Even at this difficult time, our quality practices remained unrelentingly severe. I have always told my team that quality must be a permanent standard. Many things change – customer requirement, profit and loss, and competitor products. But our quality standards must remain unaffected. During recession, production was low. We used the resources made available by this to strengthen our quality processes and R&D to develop more rigorous testing methods. No matter what the market looked like, the goods that left our stores had to be perfect. For me personally, quality has always been second nature. For my company, it has been a strict – and lucrative – business policy.

The "Limited" label had earned us greater respect. As exporters of a certain volume, we were granted export licences against which we were allotted sufficient raw material for our work. We were further entitled to import new machinery into the country, which in turn enhanced our production capacity and our ability to create new products.

Another important area in which I feel our exports helped us was product quality. To us it was extremely important to show the world what India could do. We took particular care that whatever we sent out of the country would only make us proud. Every export order we executed was constructed and tested to exceed every international specification.

All the while, we continued looking for new products to include in our range. Our major product was the PVC automobile cable, but we also produced and sold large quantities of the multipurpose flexible cables which are used in household wiring, the multi-core flexible cable used to connect household appliances, overhead axial cables, twin jumper wire for telephone cables, and many other types of cable.

Overall, we were expanding well, and our profitability was good. By the end of the financial year 1973-74, our turnover had crossed Rs. 3 crore.

1973 was also the year in which we had been blessed with another daughter, Sonali, a smiling angel of charm and sunshine.

Aruna and Prakash were quiet, well-behaved children with a few simple friends. Growing up in the middle-class Maharashtrian heartland of Prabhat Road, they were fluent in Marathi and enjoyed a meal of *varan-bhat.*

Mohini came from a very close-knit family. Her sisters Jyoti and Jayshree often came to stay with us and my children enjoyed their company a lot. During their summer holidays we took long walks to the hills nearby, enjoying the trees, birds and quiet lakes. We climbed the Hanuman Tekdi and Parvati where we visited the temple and picnicked by Pashan Lake. Sometimes we rented a bungalow in Mahableshwar and the children played and ran and cycled all day long. I enjoyed driving on long trips with my family and one year we drove all the way from Poona in our Desoto to Bangalore and then to Madurai and Kodaikanal, stopping at many places on the way. When the 1971 war in Pakistan broke out, petrol prices shot up and Mohini found it very embarrassing riding around in such a large and fancy car, so we sold it.

During the holidays we sometimes woke early and went for a walk and then for a breakfast of idli-sambar to at Vaishali restaurant, where the food was fresh and tasty. Mohini herself was an excellent cook and was famous for her delicacies which many of our friends and relatives looked forward to enjoying. Coke and Fanta were popular but to prevent our children from drinking them she would buy almonds and make thandai, a traditional cooling drink very popular in the summer months. Others laughed at her for going to so much trouble and expense, but then the drink became so sought after that she began making extra and distributing bottles, and very soon she was sending it out to all our numerous friends and relatives! Over the years, she made various kinds of squashes and pickles and distributed them, and even today, in her absence, our daughter-in-law Ritu continues the ritual, using the same traditional recipes that she had perfected. People look forward to receiving these delicacies, and in loving memory of her mother-in-law, Ritu has designed a label and sends them out with the brand "Mohini's".

Mohini was a very elegant person with a high sense of style and aesthetics and our home was always beautiful with everything in its proper place. Our children were always dressed in the best clothes and our home had the best linen and upholstery. She was also very keen on gardening. Over the years she won dozens of awards and trophies at various flower and garden shows in Poona.

Our neighbour Vasantrao Somvanshi one day told me that he had brought some grape plants from the Kolhapur-Sangli area and was thinking of taking up cultivation. He invited us to do the same. We found the idea attractive, and bought some plants from the same source, and started a small grape farm.

We later discovered that grape is a delicate crop which needs a lot of care and the Poona area is not particularly suited to it. But for the four or five years that we tended the farm, Mohini enthusiastically involved herself in its cultivation. Harvesting the grapes became a picnic for the children, and the whole family would go there on weekends. We enjoyed spending time as a family on the grape farm adjoining our factory. The children were all allotted duties and the older ones would cut the crop while the younger ones would prepare the boxes, folding and laying tissue paper inside them, and little Sonali would lie in her crib and smile and gurgle at everyone who stopped to tickle her.

I was always busy working and travelling and left the home to Mohini, who took excellent care of our home and children. Though she protected them well from our struggles and indulged them with every comfort, she also infused them with strong values of discipline, not allowing them too many mistakes. She amply compensated for my long absences by explaining my work and related pressures to the children, and giving extra importance to the occasions on which I was able to spend time with them. She managed things in such a smooth manner that they never felt anything was missing.

I sometimes wish that I had taken the time to stop and think about the way I was spending my time and set my priorities more clearly. But in those days I was just working on pure instinct, and never stopped for a single moment to consider why I was doing this or whether there were other ways to live.

I now began to believe that my life had at last settled down to one of smooth routine and comfort and I would have nothing but happiness for the rest of my days. I was soon to find out how wrong anyone can ever be to make such an impertinent assumption of this world.

5

Milwaukee, 1975
TRAGEDY - AND INNER STRENGTH

"I tend to stand by the Hindu concept of karma: that situations and opportunities come to one from one's previous history. One is then likely to automatically react in such a manner that the karma gets propagated. To avoid doing this, and to think before acting, to choose the right action instead of blindly taking an eye for an eye, one must develop a very high level of awareness and work hard to remain aware from one moment to the next. Sonali's suffering and Babaji's blessings which helped us to cope with it, are all part of my karma."

The holy city of Haridwar lies approximately 200 km to the north east of Delhi. Ever since my first trip to Haridwar in 1966, I have tried my best to make a trip there every year and spend a few days relaxing in the shadow of the magnificent, energy-giving Himalayas.

There is a bathing ghat built at the point where the Ganga leaves the Himalayas, built, by the great King Vikramaditya whose wisdom, bravery, and generosity gave rise to a very large number of legends around him. This ghat, the Har Ki Pauri, is the centre of a beautiful evening ceremony when the whole town gathers at the river banks, small diyas are floated on the water and they glide downstream, while a temple priest performs the Ganga Arti.

137

Har ki Pauri means footstep of Krishna and the name comes from a footprint embedded in a wall which is said to be that of the god Krishna. The Ganga Arti at Har ki Pauri is a spectacular and touching experience. Hundreds of people throng to the ghat to participate in this ritual every day, offering diyas and flowers that make a beautiful sight as they drift down the river. The river banks are lined with iron posts linked to each other with thick chain which bathers can hold on to so that they don't get swept away by the fast-moving river. Large orange and white towers are spaced along the banks at intervals where life-guards keep a watch on the crowded and bustling scene below. The security arrangements at Haridwar are thorough and sophisticated all the year round, and during special festive days, or during the 12-yearly Kumbh Mela, the logistics are highly complicated and meticulously planned.

The Kumbh Mela, said to be the largest religious gathering in the world, attracts millions of people on a single day.

I visited the Kumbh Mela at Haridwar in 1974. The crowd was indeed a thick press of bodies. My local contacts provided me with some amount of security and protection but the crowd was so dense that independent motion was practically impossible. The whole mass of bodies moved and somehow I found myself immersed in the Har ki Pauri Ghat and then moving out, making space for the next wave of people. To be honest, I could not understand what made the occasion special. I have always felt that the water of the Ganga that flows down from the mountain to the plains not only changes from one second to the next, but is the very same water regardless of where the sun and moon are.

It was never the ritual symbolism that attracted me to Haridwar. Neither have the frequently grimy surroundings ever kept me away. My personal experience at Haridwar, bathing in the waters of the fast-flowing icy-cold Ganga as it tumbles onto the plains after a long journey through the mountains, is one of being totally refreshed from the top of my head to the bottom of my soles, with every cell of my body radiating peace and energy. Though I don't particularly believe that sins can be washed away by this water, I gratefully acknowledge the effect this bathing experience has on me. The mountains themselves radiate peace and energy. I am filled with contentment. It is these intangibles that take me back to Haridwar year after year.

Rishikesh, 1969: Aruna and Prakash

I have never been a particularly ritualistic or superstitious person, and tend to place my faith completely in nature. As a Hindu I have visited temples in different places of pilgrimage, if I happened to be travelling on work nearby, and could conveniently visit through arrangements made by a local business contact. I don't know any prayers nor followed any rituals of fasting from my childhood, though I remember paying my respects every morning at the Jogeshwari Devi Mandir opposite our second-floor shop Ramchand Bhagwandas & Co. I have also visited Pandharpur as well as the birth places of Dnyaneshwar, Tukaram, Eknath and the other famous saints of Maharashtra. Although I am awed by the power of the tradition by which lakhs of pilgrims walk across the state every year to Pandharpur in a huge spontaneous outpouring of faith, a religious tradition spanning more than seven hundred years, it holds no personal power over me.

Over the years, I have developed respect for every spiritual school and for all types of religious thought. When I stay at my home in Goa, my driver takes me to church on Sundays. I have enjoyed visiting many important sites of worship, including Tirupati, the Meenakshi Temple in Madurai, the Ajmer Dargah, famous cathedrals of Europe, Buddha temples in Thailand and Indonesia, the Wailing Wall in Jerusalem, and many more. Until recently, I used to make these pilgrimages once in every few months with a group of friends which include Mohini's brother Ramesh and his wife Laltu, my daughter Aruna and her husband Mukesh. Mohini's sister Jayshree and her husband Prakash who live in the U.S. would often join us on these trips.

I have met many spiritually great people including Shankaracharya of the Kanchi Math, Chinmayananda Swami, Satya Sai Baba, Swaminarayan, Prabhupad, Rajneesh, the Mother of the Aurobindo Ashram, and many more. I have certainly benefited from the time spent with them. The well-known Anandmayee Ma temple is very close to my present home. Soon after we moved here, Mohini and I met the renowned spiritual guru Anandmayee Ma and she even graced our home with her presence. She later made me President of her ashram trust, requesting me to hold the position as long as I live, and I have done so for the last 41 years.

However, I was never driven by the thought that I must visit a particular place because it is a festival day or pooja. By and large, my life experience has taught me that when one works with complete dedication and immerses oneself in the task without any thought for reward, guidance and answers come automatically, as if from some external source.

In the year 1974, I was fortunate enough to meet another person who formed, for me, the embodiment of that external source and became my living guide and mentor, helping and comforting me through one of the most difficult phases of my life. This was the saintly Swami Ram Baba. Known to his disciples with love and devotion as Param Pujya Paramhans Shri Swami Ram Baba, Babaji was originally from a royal family of Rajasthan. He graduated from Cambridge University, and later turned to deep study of the ancient Vedic texts, and became famous for his knowledge in these areas, particularly in the Yoga Sutras of Patanjali. In 1910 Babaji was given a mystic initiation into sainthood by Swami Shankaranand on the bank of the Ganga at Karanbas, a small village in U.P. not far from Delhi. He was given the name Swami Vigyananand, and, as his guru instructed, became a wandering mendicant.

After about two years of this life Babaji came across a nameless yogi, one of those enlightened souls who have completed all the cycles of existence and have taken birth on the earth once more for the mere purpose of the bliss of existence. He sat silent in meditation, but there was a mystic bond between the two.

Only a very few words passed between them. This great person, known only by the title Shri Nagababa Mahapurusha, advised Babaji on his spiritual journey, instructing him to give up the name Vigyanand, and to live his life as guru without ever building an ashram, and without ever looking back at what he had left behind. "Go ahead dedicatedly, sincerely, and without any ego – even of your Sadhana, your spiritual practice," he was told. Babaji followed these instructions faithfully.

The story goes that in early 1913, Swami Ram Baba received a mystic call to visit Shirdi in search of Sai Baba. In those days this travel was extremely difficult, but providence made miraculous arrangements in the form of a group of princes who were travelling there and agreed to take Babaji with them.

At Shirdi, he approached the mosque where the great saint was sitting, and noticed that he was eating dry rotis and onion. The scornful thought arose in his mind that a person eating a meal as crude as this could be of no help to him in his meditation. Sai Baba looked at him and spoke aloud, "One who can digest a meal such as this must only eat such food!"

This incident has been retold many times. It is important not only in the history of Sai Baba's chronology of sainthood as an example of a public occasion when Sai Baba knew what another person was thinking without a single word spoken. It is also important because it encourages every seeker to understand that even a soul at the level of evolution of Swami Ram Baba can still fall prey to destructive thoughts from the ego. The reassuring message is that we are all human beings, all in the same boat, all victims of the same destructive ego within. We must all work to conquer it without ceasing. We must never, ever feel complacent that we have conquered ego – the very thought arises from nowhere but ego!

It is said that on this occasion, Sai Baba gazed intently into Swami Ram Baba's eyes and from that moment onwards, his ego sizzled to a cinder, and he became enlightened.

In today's world, it is extremely difficult to find a guru.

Firstly, concepts such as renunciation, previous births, and self-realisation might seem alien to those immersed in a materialistic world of labels, brands, and intoxication to substance of various kinds. However, even today, there are many who wear orange robes and live the life of a yogi. They are simply seekers, like you and me, but their commitment to the path is visibly symbolised by their renunciation of worldly life. There are yet others on the path of enlightenment who are recognized as wise gurus, who seek followers and pass on their wisdom in an organized manner, building up cults who worship them.

To find a simple, great soul like Swami Ram Baba, willing to give his guidance to ordinary individuals on a one-to-one basis without any thought for reward, however, is practically impossible. Such a person would never go out looking for you. You would just have to be lucky enough to find him. And it is one of the greatest blessings of my life that I was lucky enough to do so.

It so happened that at 8.30 p.m. one day in 1974, I received a phone call from Anantrao Shinde. He was at that time Manager in charge of Administration and Labour Welfare at Finolex. Mr. Shinde informed me that Swami Ram Baba had arrived and was staying with him, and he was keen that I should meet him. I had just returned home after a long day at work, and had to get up early to leave for Bombay next morning. It was the middle of July with rains pouring heavily. The Mumbai-Pune Express Highway was still more than thirty years in the future and the drive to Bombay would take more than five hours in this weather. After working all day in Bombay next day, I was scheduled to fly to London at night. To prepare for the long day ahead, I had intended to retire early.

However, Mr. Shinde had mentioned Swami Ram Baba before and I had been curious, and definitely interested in meeting him. After thinking about it for a while, I decided to go. Mohini and I had dinner, put the children to bed, and drove out to Yeshwant Nagar where Mr. Shinde had a bungalow.

The moment I saw Swami Ram Baba, I felt an immediate response from within. It was an internal communication which is hard to describe, so strong and joyous that it was tangible in my mind, in my heart and throughout my body. We spoke for some time and I knew even after this very short meeting that our association was already important to me and that it would continue for a very long time, as long as we lived, even after that. Right from the first meeting, our relationship was one of tremendous warmth and intensity.

As we took leave to return home I told him that I was going to be away, and requested him to visit my home and bless my children. Mohini offered to make all the necessary arrangements. However, when I returned home a few weeks later, she told me that Babaji had come on his own, using public transport, and spent time with the children who had all been very drawn to him and enjoyed his company greatly. At this time, Aruna was fifteen, Prakash was eleven, and Sonali was a baby about a year old.

Sonali was born on the 3rd of July 1973, at Breach Candy Hospital in Bombay. It was a day I will always remember. With heavy rains, the roads were flooding and the traffic was congested and sluggish as only

Bombay traffic in the middle of the monsoon can be. I had been familiar with Bombay from my early days of working in the electrical accessories trading business. Later as well, I visited Bombay often on government work or to go to the airport. My in-laws also lived in Bombay. In 1967 I had purchased an office near Opera House for our operations, and few years later bought a flat for my youngest brother Narayan at Warden Road when he began managing our Bombay office. The hospital where Sonali was born was in a low-lying area and as the surrounding roads were water logged, it was difficult to access. Just travelling from the hospital to the office or N.P.'s flat took nearly an hour each way.

All of us were delighted to welcome this new addition to our family. She was very sweet and we adored her as a small doll, a tiny bundle to be loved and petted always. When she laughed, it was such a charming sound that it made us all happy. She blessed our lives with a new and totally unexpected dimension of joy. When Aruna and Prakash had been born, our lives were just beginning and it was a time of struggle and hardship. Our circumstances had improved steadily and our level of comfort and prosperity had grown. I now had more time and leisure to enjoy the company of my children. It was a special gift to have an adored baby whom we could watch as she grew from an infant and slowly started walking and talking. I remember Sonali when she was a baby less than a year old sitting next to me during my singing lessons with my masterji. She would watch me and lift her hand in imitation and Mohini and I would laugh in delight. While the older children did their homework, they could take a break and to cuddle or play with her.

I continued to meet Swami Ram Baba in Bombay and then again in Poona. After discussing the matter with Mohini, I invited Babaji to stay with us at our home on Prabhat Road Galli No. 11. We were very happy when he consented and, on a visit to our city at the end of 1974, he graced our home with a visit.

We had an intense bond, a feeling of warmth that I had never experienced in my life before. I discussed every matter under the sun with him, relying on his wisdom for suggestions and guidance. It is difficult to explain the feeling a shishya or student can have for a guru. It is something that one must experience and feel for oneself.

It was interesting to host this great personality in other ways as well. People visited him from all over the country. Our home was filled with his devotees from early morning till late at night. I have no idea how they knew he was in Poona, and staying in our home. It seemed that there were many others like myself who had felt the same magnetic attraction and sense of well-being he generated. He would talk to each person who came to see him, giving his full energy and attention, and soothing them as they poured out their concerns. He often apologized to my wife, who besides the duties of the house and the care of baby Sonali, had to attend to all his visitors. However for us, it was a pleasure and an honour.

I remember one evening when we had a visit from a Gujarati gentleman Dr. Modi, who was a tantric. He was in conversation with Swami Ram Baba and I heard him say something to indicate that my family and I would soon be spending a lot of time in the U.S. I was about to ask what he meant when Babaji gestured him to keep silent. I was puzzled, since I had no connection with the U.S. There was no possibility that I would expand my operations to cover that country in any way. It was not long before I found out what Dr. Modi had meant. However, another very important event in my life was to occur before that.

In 1975, I was initiated by Swami Ram Baba as a disciple, with the full traditional mystic Hindu initiation rites used for such purposes since Vedic times.

I remember the day I asked Babaji whether he could initiate me. He burst out laughing. "You are talking somebody else's language!" he said. I felt a little embarrassed because he was right, as usual. Someone else had suggested to me that I ask Babaji for initiation. I had no idea what that was and had asked him to write down the word which he did, in both Hindi and English. I had stared at the word for a while, and later asked others what it meant, but no one could give a satisfactory explanation. I gathered that it was some type of ceremony at which a name or a mantra would be given. However, I kept silent and was surprised when a few months later Babaji himself told me that he would perform the initiation on my birthday.

He now began to make solemn preparations. It was to be a ritual lasting two hours. He ordered special items for the ritual, what we call pooja samagri, from a shop in Bombay. He told Mohini that he would perform the initiation in the dining room and he would need complete silence with no interruptions. We removed the dining table from the room, and made arrangements for Sonali to be looked after by our dear friends and neighbours the Rathis.

Leaving strict instructions that there should be no noise or disturbance for the entire two-hour period, Babaji honoured me with his initiation. It was an experience that shook my body and soul and changed my life completely. It seemed as if Babaji had transferred some of his spiritual energy, his own store of precious karmically earned spiritual energy, to me. The strong vibrations of the event and the smell of sandalwood and other pooja items remained in our home for several months. Many of our neighbours inquired what the aroma was.

After the ceremony Babaji told me that chanting and prayers were all very well, but I should continue to work; that work was my meditation.

I did continue to work as before, leaving home early morning and returning after a full day's work, but there was a new intensity to all my experiences which helped me to concentrate and perform better. My actions were smoother and my decisions came simply and without too much worry or juggling of options.

I also continued to travel as before. However, I now felt myself in a state of perpetual meditation. The mantra he had bestowed on me was in my mind continuously. I also became closer to Babaji and was able to communicate with him at any time, even when we were physically in different locations. If I was undecided about something, or if I had a question, I would mentally ask Babaji. The answer always came. I had not been brought up in the tradition of guru and disciple. For someone with my upbringing to have a guru was unusual. Babaji always said that it was not I who had chosen him but rather that I was his choice. He had personally selected me to give comfort and guidance to.

One day after I returned home from a trip abroad, Mohini told me that Babaji had recently predicted that we would soon buy a house. She said he had closed his eyes and described a beautiful, fully furnished bungalow on two acres of land. I laughed. The thought was very amusing because I knew I had no money and there was absolutely no chance of my buying a house of this type in the near future.

It so happened that some time after this, I was introduced to a Dr. Manohar V. Shirodkar at a social occasion in Bombay.

His father had been one of the leading gynaecologist in India with a nursing home at Cumballa Hill, Bombay, and an international reputation for a surgical procedure known as the "Shirodkar knot" which is still used to treat cervical incontinence.

When we met, Dr. Manohar casually told me that he had a house in Poona which he had been thinking of selling. Just as casually, I asked him what he was expecting for it. He told me that it was at 9 ICS Colony, near the Poona University, set in around two acres of land, and he expected something in the region of Rs. 5 lakh. It was occupied by a German couple associated with the Max Mueller Bhavan.

As soon as I returned to Poona, I told Mohini about this place and we drove out to see it with our children. It was a large bungalow surrounded by tall trees, green lawns and pleasantly isolated. All of us liked it very much and became excited at the prospect of owning and living in this beautiful wooded house! I now began trying to contact Manohar to complete the sale. He and his mother lived in different areas of Bombay and for the next several months, I tried in vain to arrange a meeting between the three of us to arrive at an agreement.

Around this time, R.P. suddenly took ill in Kuwait and was admitted in hospital with a heart attack. I rushed to Kuwait with Dr. B.K. Goel, the eminent Bombay cardiologist, to make sure that he was well looked after. When I returned, Mohini greeted me with the news that Mrs. Shirodkar senior had visited our home and spent time with her, and had agreed to sell the place to us. The previous tenants had terminated their lease and the house was unoccupied, so we could collect the keys to the bungalow from her security guard, who would hand over charge of the house to our security guard.

I was delighted, of course, but also worried about where we would get the money to pay for it! However, by the time I raised Rs. 40,000 for the initial payment and sent it across, they had already handed over the keys and possession of the house and all its contents to us without a single paisa or any document exchanged. I was able to pay the remaining money to the family only in instalments, and that too over a period of nearly two years. It was the most pleasant, friendly and generous land deal anyone could imagine. All of us, Mohini, Aruna, Prakash and baby Sonali who was now two, and I were simply delighted.

Today I live in the same bungalow with Prakash and his wife Ritu and and my two sweet granddaughters Gayatri, whose pet name is Prakita, and Hansika-Hiya, who we usually call Hansu. Though we have made a few changes to the house, we are lucky that it continues to be in a quiet, leafy, residential area with very little traffic.

Towards the end of that year, Babaji told us that we must think of moving into the new house soon. If we did not, he said, there would be a delay on my birthday.

It was a fine-looking house, and we all looked forward to moving in and making it our home. The garden was badly overrun, but it was surrounded by beautiful old trees and this was a source of delight for all of us. We all looked forward to planning and creating a neat and attractive garden. Before we moved into the house, there was also a lot of scrubbing and painting to be done. It was a rambling building with many rooms, and as Babaji had foretold, it was fully furnished. A lot of the furniture was old; solid antique wood and brass. The kitchen was fully stocked with utensils of all kinds. Many of the rooms were locked and were used as warehouses for costly items, silverware, Chinese porcelain, and antiques.

Dr. Shirodkar senior had been greatly revered and for more than fifty years he had been the continuous recipient of gifts from the grateful husbands of patients he had performed his miracles for – maharajahs, expatriates, and wealthy individuals from every community. Mohini had all these items taken out and cleaned, and she gave most of them away as gifts to others. We had decided not to open the whole house but to use just the few rooms that we needed for the time being. Mohini began the process of scrubbing, painting, floor-polishing, upholstery and so on. Finally, a few months later, we moved into the house in early March.

Housewarming pooja, 1977: Parvatibai (mother)
with P. P. Chhabria

It was now the 12th of March 1977, my birthday, and we were ready for a small housewarming celebration with few of our friends and relatives. That evening, Sonali was unwell and restless. She cried continuously, seemingly in pain. One of our guests was Dr. Anand Pandit, the well-known child specialist and I requested him to come upstairs and examine her.

After spending some time with Sonali, Dr. Pandit suggested that we send a blood sample to the haematology clinic of a Dr. Arvind Marathe at Rasta Peth, one of the few laboratories in Poona at that time. We did so first thing next morning. By afternoon we had the reports. Sonali had been diagnosed with leukaemia.

Through the haze of horror and disbelief, I became aware that this was the reason Babaji had told us to move to the new house immediately or there would be a delay. I also thought back to the occasion on which the Gujarati tantric Dr. Modi had discussed our imminent visit to the U.S. with Babaji, and I now understood what it meant. They had seen some invisible sign on Sonali which told them that she was destined to suffer a serious illness.

All of us were stunned. Sonali had been born in our family after a gap of ten years. We all loved her very much and the other children in the family enjoyed playing with her and petting her as if she was their doll. It was very painful to think that she was suffering a life-threatening illness.

Medical facilities in those days were better in the U.S. than they were here, and for our beloved child to have a chance at the best treatment, we would have to take her there.

I felt lost and confused. K.P., who had stood by my side all these years, was away in Iran, providing the technology to build a pipe factory for a Sikh industrialist there. Our factory was in a high-growth phase and needed my constant time and attention. What could I do?

Mohini and I decided that it would be unbearable for our family to be separated at this point. Aruna and Prakash's respective schools were most understanding and granted them leaves of absence. The children all had

Sonali, 1977: Already ailing

to have passports made. It was quite easy to obtain passports and visas, and these procedures did not add to our agony as they would have in today's world.

Through my doctor friends I had been advised that the best medical treatment for Sonali would be at Milwaukee, under a Dr. Donald Pinkel who specialised in children's leukaemia. Though Milwaukee had just a small county hospital, Dr. Pinkel was considered a miracle worker, and had founded the Midwest Children's Cancer Centre. He was a specialist in the disease Sonali had been diagnosed with; Acute Lymphoblastic Leukaemia, and it was under his guidance that a "can do" approach had evolved towards the cure of ALL. At this time Dr. Pinkel was Pediatrician-in-chief at Milwaukee Children's Hospital. Leukaemia was not a well-researched illness and we were very fortunate that Dr. Marathe had spotted it and given us the best chance we had for early treatment.

It was April 1977 when our family, accompanied by Mohini's brother Ramesh Menda, set off for the U. S. When we landed in Milwaukee, we were warmly greeted. The hospital assigned us to an apartment nearby at a nominal rent. We could cook our own food.

Sonali's treatment began.

There weren't many Indians in the U.S., only about twelve or fifteen Indian families in all of Milwaukee. Nowadays, every Indian community has its own association in Milwaukee but back then, it was just the Indian Association.

The first to visit us were Gul Advani and his wife Premu. They had heard that an Indian family had brought their cancer-afflicted daughter for treatment to their city. They arrived carrying big containers filled with home-cooked Sindhi food.

It is just unbelievable to think that this was our very first trip to the U.S. All of a sudden we were surrounded by friends and had become the centre of a warm and loving community.

Premu cooked both lunch and dinner for us every weekend. There were so many smiling, caring faces around us that the grim reality of Sonali's daily treatment was greatly softened.

Since I had been a Rotarian in Poona, I decided to attend a meeting of the local Rotary Club. After the meeting, while we were standing and chatting, a gentleman came and introduced himself. He was Reuben Peterson and he worked in a solicitor's firm. When I told him about my daughter's treatment he said he would like to bring his family to visit us. That weekend, he and his wife Patti and their five children came to see us in our small apartment. They took us for a drive and later we went to their home for dinner. I had heard that Americans were formal and lived a fast-paced life which had no room for friendship or acts of generosity. What a mistaken notion!

When Patti heard about my work and the fact that my mother was alone at home, she suggested to me that I could now go back to Poona and she would make sure Mohini and Sonali were well looked after. By now she was calling my wife Mona, and often took Sonali and her out shopping and sightseeing and bought them gifts. "We are here," she told me. "Don't worry about a thing! You can go back if you want."

I took Aruna and Prakash and went home while Mohini stayed behind with Sonali in the care of the Petersons. When the doctors told us that Sonali was in remission, I flew back to Milwaukee to bring my wife and daughter home. The Petersons decided to celebrate the good news. They invited several of their friends and gave us a big send-off party in their home.

A few months later, Babaji and I were taking our evening stroll in the grounds of my bungalow in Poona. Mohini's younger sister Jayshree was spending a few days with us. Babaji told me to get a passport made for her.

I was puzzled, but had long stopped questioning him and started the proceedings for her passport immediately. I had learnt that Babaji was one of those exceptional beings with powers beyond the normal range of human abilities, and could see things that we could not. There was much that was clearly evident to him that was not yet manifest, or was hidden from us in other ways.

Within a few days, the family received a marriage proposal for Jayshree from a boy in Toledo, Ohio. He was a doctor, and arrangements were made for them to meet in Bombay. The two liked each other and preparations for the wedding began.

Life continued as usual at home but when Sonali developed fever again, Dr. Marathe informed us that there had been a relapse and advised us to return to Milwaukee and continue treatment, with Dr. Pinkel, and the weekly therapy.

We now decided that Mohini and I would take Sonali to the U.S., and my mother would look after Aruna and Prakash while we were away.

It was now mid-December and bitterly cold. This time we flew via New York instead of Chicago. Due to heavy snowfall our flight was delayed and we missed our connection to Milwaukee. It seemed as if the weather had decided to add to our misery. It was so bad that we were not able to enter the city and stayed at a small hotel with no amenities, close to the airport. Sonali was crying with hunger and exhaustion, and with some difficulty I managed to get bread, butter and milk for her and put her to bed. Mohini and I stayed up all night and we flew to Milwaukee next day. Here too it was snowbound and our friends had been unable to drive to the airport to pick us up. With difficulty we found a taxi and drove straight to the hospital. We were now told that Sonali would have to be given radiation. This was still a primitive form of treatment, sometimes with terrible side-effects. One of Dr. Pinkel's team members came to me with a consent form. I was told that there was a possibility that the radiation could make Sonali blind. Mohini and I were shocked and did not know how to react. When I returned to the apartment, I was surprised to receive a phone call from Babaji. It must have been midnight in India. Before I could explain our dilemma, he said to me, "Don't worry, just go ahead with what they are telling you to do." With this assurance, I signed the form and the treatment proceeded.

I had always noticed that even his phone calls came through effortlessly. When I tried to make a call from India to the U.S., it would take hours on end. Quite often the operator would call late at night to say there was no line available and we would postpone the call to the next day. But his alignment with the forces of the universe was so simple and comfortable that when he wanted to speak to someone – he just did.

154

Milwaukee, 1978: Dr. Prakash, Jayshree, Swami Ram Baba,
Sonali, Mohini and P. P.

I would call a private taxi in the morning to take Sonali to the county hospital in Milwaukee for the radiation treatment. On the way back, we used the public transport which cost only one dollar because we had a hospital card. When I think back, I feel overcome with sadness that I had troubled my child in her illness and suffering, travelling in the bitter Milwaukee cold of −15°C by bus rather than taxi, just to save a few dollars.

On some days Sonali seemed better, and we would all feel happy and pray for a miracle. But on the days when we could see her suffering, it was a terrible thing for all of us. We prayed continuously for her recovery. We watched her become thin, and waste away before our eyes. The treatment made her weak and cranky.

One of the things that cheered us all up was that we now had family of our own in addition to all the friends we had made in Milwaukee. Mohini's sister Jayshree and her newly-wedded husband Dr. Prakash Chhabria (who by a coincidence had the same name as my son) came and spent many weekends with us. Sonali was very attached to Jayshree. The first weekend they spent in Milwaukee, she refused to let her go back. Jayshree stayed on, and Dr. Prakash drove home to Toledo on his own. Dr. Prakash had specialised in radiology, so we relied on him for medical advice and Sonali's care as well.

They say that the only one who can love a child as much as the mother is the masi, and it was a strange twist of destiny for Jayshree to be taken from Bombay to the U.S. to give her baby niece special love and care in her time of suffering and need. Many people have helped me in my life, and Dr. Prakash is one of those who did the most, giving his time and effort with such unconditional generosity that I will always consider him to be one of those closest to me. None of us will ever forget the force of the selfless love and support that our whole family received from the two of them, going so much out of their way to be with us and help us so soon after their marriage. They continued the long road drives even when Jayshree was expecting a baby of her own.

Jayshree and Dr. Prakash later settled in Milwaukee, and till today it is a routine that I enjoy a holiday with them there every year.

Milwaukee, 1978 :
Patti Peterson with Sonali

Milwaukee, 1978:
Premu Advani, Sonali and Mohini

It was now March 1978. I began worrying about what was happening at the factory. We needed revenue. Besides, the company was expanding fast and needed my direction and involvement.

Swami Ram Baba now offered to stay in Milwaukee with my daughter so that I could return to Poona.

We made arrangements for his travel and it was while the necessary documents were being processed that we discovered his date of birth to be the 22nd of February 1860, which meant that at this time Babaji was 118 years old!

In Milwaukee, he took a room in the hotel next to my family. Knowing that he was there to soothe and comfort Sonali throughout her treatment, I was able to go back home and concentrate on my work. He stayed there for nearly four months. His participation in her treatment was a great comfort and help to my family and me as a result to the growth of my organization as well.

Alone at home, I would lie awake at night thinking to myself that this was a period in which we should have been granted happiness and peace. After so many years of moving from one small flat to another, managing with the most basic amenities, we were finally in our own beautiful new bungalow, one of the best and most luxurious properties in Poona at that time. The entire family, my children, my mother, sisters and brothers had all been so happy for us. But then we had received this sudden shock.

After tossing and turning all night, I would fall asleep by morning and after just a few short hours it would be time to get up and go to work. Towards the end of 1978 I had to travel to Milwaukee for a third time to bring my family back to India. This time there was a crisis in the factory and I went via Iran so that I could meet K.P. who was still supervising the construction of the pipe factory there and apprise him of the situation.

Our Finance Controller & Company Secretary, Mr. M.Y. Paranjape, had submitted his resignation. Paranjpe had been with us for many years. I had personally hired him from Bank of India and we had worked closely together. He had played an important role during the merger of Alfa Rubber and Indian Cable Industries, staying up late with Mr. Mysore and Mr. Bhide to complete the documentation. It was he who had presented me with my sitar.

His sudden decision came as a great shock. He was the most senior person in the company and critical to our operations at this juncture when I myself was immersed in a personal tragedy and absent from work for long periods of time. But even more shocking was the fact that several others had got together with him and they had jointly put in their papers.

K.P. had to be informed of this and I stopped over for two days in Iran on my way to Milwaukee to bring Sonali back. It seemed as if these people had all lost confidence in us because of the personal problems I was facing, and felt that they had nothing to gain by staying on in a company that, to their minds, was on the verge of collapse.

My biggest support at this time was Babaji's constant reassurance. "People may try to pressurise you, but don't worry!" he would say. "Everything will work out." It was this that saved me from diluting my energy with worry, serene that I had his blessing, and it gave me the calm strength and confidence to continue working, even when it was just K.P. and me alone, to restore the company with full force.

Babaji constantly reminded me that we must focus our energy and attention in the present. "The past is over," he would say, "we can't change it! The future is not known, why worry about it? Work with faith and patience in the present!"

When I returned to Poona, I immediately began looking for good senior people. In a few months I had appointed Mr. G.S. Talauliker, also from Bank of India. He joined as Executive Director, and over a period of several months we brought in a new and dynamic team in every division of the company. During my first trip to Milwaukee, I had requested Dr. Pinkel to provide special training to Dr. Arvind Marathe in his laboratory so that he could serve other needy children in Poona. I had seen how difficult it was for a family whose beloved member was ill with this horrible illness. Though we were not rich, somehow money came to us when we needed it, and I kept thinking of the many poor people who had no hope at all and who would lose their children to leukaemia only because they had no access to funds.

We made arrangements for Dr. Marathe's passport and other necessary documents, and I purchased a ticket for him to travel to Milwaukee. He had relatives in the city with whom he was able to stay during this period.

Dr. Pinkel was a great man and he was happy to give Dr. Marathe the knowledge and expertise to help other children in Poona. He also trained him on the use of new laboratory equipment, which I purchased for him to bring back to Poona.

In 1979, the Year of the Child, I formalised this arrangement by setting up a trust aimed at helping needy children get cancer aid. It was a difficult decision because large expense was involved. However, I did feel entitled to spend what I was personally earning. I discussed the matter with Swami Ram Baba and he encouraged me to go ahead and try to make some provision for poor families when this dreaded disease came. I put up Rs. 20,000 and Babaji named it the Hope Foundation, a name that we all liked and felt was appropriate for what we wanted it to represent. Today we have a small laboratory at Jungli Maharaj Road where free treatment is provided to needy people. Doctors know the Hope Foundation and send patients with recommendations for medicine as required. The Hope Foundation has now added education to the scope of its activities, ranging from primary right up to the postgraduate level.

Right through 1979 and 1980 it seemed as if Sonali was improving, and her blood count was reassuring. However in August 1981 she had a sudden relapse. We consulted many doctors. All the while, Mohini hoped and prayed that one day Sonali would be cured. But it seemed that the disease had gone too deep. The doctors could only give a ten to fifteen percent chance of recovery.

Dr. Marathe would have to test her bone marrow every week, extracting it from her spine with a fine needle and she would scream in agony. It was a terrible thing for the whole family.

Swami Ram Baba was on the road from Nasik to Shirdi, and he placed a trunk call to talk to me, inquiring about Sonali's blood count. I told him that she was ill and suffering.

Babaji now asked me whether I had decided to take her back to the U.S. At that moment I took a decision. "I don't want to torture her any more," I told him. "No, we are not going back." Aspirating her bone marrow had been the most horrible experience. She would shout and scream in pain. I now decided that we would give her gentle treatment at home with homoeopathic medication and every comfort that we could provide her ourselves. This was a big decision to make, but once we did, we all felt better. We realised that her life was in the hands of God and that we could only try to relieve her agony as best as we could until the final moment came.

It was the 3rd of September 1981 when we finally lost our beloved child. Dr. B. N. Gurjar, a highly skilled homoeopathic doctor, was a good friend of ours and he had been treating Sonali all through her illness. He now visited daily. Babaji came to visit us every few weeks. When he touched her to give his blessing, we could see that the pain had gone and Sonali felt peaceful. Sometimes she even laughed with joy.

It was evening, around 6 o'clock on the day before Anant Chaturdashi, the final immersion day of the Ganesh festival. Sonali was in our room, and we were lying peacefully on the diwan watching TV. All of a sudden, she insisted that we take her inside. She wanted to lie in her own bed. I tried to convince her that we wanted her here, but she was very vehement about wanting to go back. Soon after I took her back to her room, she went into a coma.

Babaji was staying with us. He had arrived just two days before. Perhaps he knew that this was going to happen. I immediately thought of going to call him but before I could do so, he came upstairs. We called Dr. Gurjar, and the four of us sat by her side for a few hours. At around 10.30 Babaji told us to go ahead and have our dinner and he would take care of her, but Mohini refused to leave her side. Finally Babaji was the one to get up saying that he would come back when the time came. At around 2 o'clock he woke me up and we went to the room where Sonali lay with Mohini sitting next to her.

It was 4.30 when Babaji opened all the doors and windows. It was a full-moon night and her bed was floodlit with the Anant Chaturdashi moon. He bent down and whispered something into Sonali's ear. She opened her eyes and Mohini and I saw her looking at us for a split second, and we both clearly heard her say "Hare Ram". Her legs swung around abruptly to face south. In the moonlight, I saw a white flash of light as Sonali's soul left her body.

One may feel that a sight like this comes from culture, or tradition, or religious belief, or from the subconscious, but the fact is that I saw and heard it with my own eyes and ears. Once again I experienced the evidence of Babaji's saintly nature.

It was a week day. Through our overwhelming sorrow, we trembled at the thought of having to inform Prakash who loved his younger sister with the kind of special love that one can only feel for a small child. Prakash was away in the U.S. at that time studying for his B.S. He used to phone us every weekend to tell us his news and ask about us. He knew how critically ill Sonali was and was deeply concerned. It would have been difficult for us to phone him with the bad news, because he would have been at school and the phone was in a building some distance away, at a common place from where the students would call each other.

That day, somehow, Prakash himself called. He had had a dream about Sonali and was phoning to ask how she was. We had to give him the sad news which left him shattered with grief, so far away from home.

My brother Kishan carried Sonali's body in his arms to the Vaikunth crematorium near Lakdi Pul and her final rites were performed . Though saints and mystics normally never associate themselves with cremation rites, Babaji had loved my daughter so much that he now came forward himself and arranged all the formalities. We decided to take the ashes to Haridwar and Babaji accompanied our group which included Aruna, Dr. Gurjar and my eldest brother B.P. and his wife Sulochana. Mohini's elder sister Sushila is like a mother figure to the whole family. She and her husband Gobindram Makhija also accompanied us to Haridwar on this sad journey.

The day after the ceremony, we travelled to nearby Rishikesh which has a long tradition of being one of the holy places in our country, with many temples and ashrams. I was having a dip in the water when Babaji suddenly called me. He anointed me with Ganga water, flowers and rice, and said something in my ear. "I have given you whatever I had," he told me.

Soon after we returned to Poona, he gave me the beej mantra, a kind of post doctorate of the initiation ceremony. I had mentioned to him some years before that I was keen to take this next powerful step on the spiritual journey, and he had said to me in his cryptic way, "The fruit must be ripe, only then can I pick it." We had subsequently never discussed it, but now this milestone too had been quietly crossed.

Sonali's illness had affected the lives of each of us in the family. We were all depressed by this tragic turn our lives had taken. During the entire period, the only thought in our minds was what would happen to our darling. We had all been so fond of her, and after she was diagnosed, we became completely devoted to her comfort. During this period of four years, time stood still for Aruna and Prakash as well. They were at an age when they should have been enjoying themselves in college with their friends, perhaps doing courses or engaging in part-time occupations which would have laid the foundation for skills they would use in their later lives. For much of this time Prakash was away studying, first in the U.K. and then in the U.S., but for Aruna in particular, those were years of the spring of her youth lost forever.

The others in our family, my brothers and sisters and Mohini's brothers and sisters, had done their best to comfort and support us in our sorrow. Ramesh and Laltu were now living in Dubai. Ramesh travelled with us to the U.S. and came to visit us frequently while we were there, and Laltu had made any number of trips to Poona to stay with Aruna and Prakash, take care of the house, and cheer them up.

My wife and I were not in the habit of going to parties and social events and now we stopped going out completely. Mohini had stayed in the U.S. for long stretches of time. There she had managed all the housework herself, something she had not been used to, having always had servants in India. I was unable to concentrate on my work. There were days when I would leave the house to go to the factory. Halfway I would change my mind and tell the driver to turn around because I wanted to be with my daughter. To see your child suffering and wasting away before your eyes brings a tearing, desperate unhappiness. After we lost Sonali, Mohini was overcome with a grief that never completely left her. After that, till the end of her days, she never went out of the house to meet anyone or enjoyed celebrations of any kind. She never complained and continued to live and work as she had before, but there was something vital missing and she too died an untimely death which, the doctors said, could have arisen from self-neglect and the type of never-ending sorrow that can shorten one's life. During Sonali's illness my music lessons had been discontinued. I had been singing ever since I was very young and had been playing the sitar also for a few years. Singing was something I enjoyed and could lose myself in completely. Even though when I sang, I was singing someone else's songs, I could still feel the joy of creativity in the melody and in the expression. After Sonali died, I stopped singing.

Throughout this sad period of our lives, it was Babaji's presence that gave us comfort and strength. All the while there was the feeling that there was somebody with us, watching us, blessing us. This helped us to continue looking after Sonali without breaking down. It helped us to realise that when suffering comes, it must be faced and that life must go on and that we must choose the right action and make the right decision with full awareness from one moment to the next.

Swami Ram Baba was a giant of a man, 6'8" in height. Despite his great and unbelievable age of 118, he was in perfect health and walked at a speed that young men found hard to keep up with. When someone came to see him, he would close his eyes and know what the person had come for, what he wanted, and the events of his life – not just past and present but future also. He never thrust this information forward, but waited for the person to speak. He lived among us like an ordinary person, eating one meal a day along with the family. But there would be days on which he would take leave from us and go into retreat. He would request us not to disturb him for anything. After many days without food or even water, and often at the moment when I most needed him for something, he would appear just as suddenly. Sometimes he would say, "I am tired, I have travelled so far!"

Babaji never spoke about his early life. When we were together I never wondered who he was or where he had come from. I knew who he was from deep within, and I accepted all that he said and did and understood its value and felt highly privileged to be associated with him. These days since I have some free time to reflect, and I have gathered a few facts about him from many sources. A lot of it is guesswork. He never initiated any discussion on politics or economics or business, but would respond easily to questions in any of these areas. He was a very knowledgeable person and had travelled widely and visited many countries and had even been to Saudi Arabia, Mecca and Medina. He had no religion but could chant prayers of every faith. He answered questions in any area and helped people with every conceivable problem that they faced in their lives. He spoke to us about simple ways of living. And he often talked to us about other holy men and women who had achieved enlightenment. His philosophy was not based on any religion but on practical wisdom.

Paramhans is a title bestowed on enlightened teachers in Hinduism, and literally translates as "supreme swan". The saying goes that these beings have achieved the highest purity of body, that when they drink water, it comes out as water; when they drink milk – it comes out as milk.

I have met many holy and enlightened people and always felt some benefit from the meeting. Just as water flows from a higher to a lower level, ordinary people always benefit from meeting someone at a higher level of consciousness. One thing I noticed they all had in common was that they were extremely simple and don't show off or try to push themselves forward.

I tend to stand by the Hindu concept of karma: that situations and opportunities come to one from one's previous history. One is then likely to automatically react in such a manner that the karma gets propagated. To avoid doing this, and to think before acting, to choose the right action instead of blindly taking an eye for an eye, one must develop a very high level of awareness, and work hard to remain aware from one moment to the next. Sonali's suffering, and Babaji's blessings which helped us to cope with it, are all part of my karma. I had no money but I was able to make arrangements to take Sonali to the U.S. for treatment. Before that, with just Rs. 40,000 at my disposal, we had been able to move into a home that was worth a great deal more. Every time my company had been ready for expansion, land had come to us like a gift from heaven.

There have been so many people in my life who appeared suddenly, and gave me unexpected and timely help. When the flood destroyed much of Pune, our irreplaceable machinery had already been moved to safety.

I have learnt to look at every situation and decision of my life in the context of karmic reactions, karmic give-and-take, and always try to respond with awareness to break the chain of karma in any situation. Babaji always told us that in life you must give something. Only then you can think of yourself. I never look back and wish things had been different or regret anything. I never spent time thinking that if my father had not died when I was twelve years old how different things would have been. I believe in today, in the present moment.

In my life, I have lost many who are dear to me, my father, my grandmother, my mother, my daughter, my baby grandson, and my wife. The pain of their loss is still sharp and vivid. When I remember them, I look up and gaze into the sky, wondering whether, wherever they are, they can feel the message of love that I continue to send to them. No matter how much pain I felt at their loss, I never cried in public.

I did not shed a single tear even when Babaji left me. He took Samadhi in 1989, on Shiv Ratri, a moonless night in February, the anniversary of the day on which Shiva is said to have performed the Tandava Nritya, the dance of primordial creation, preservation and destruction. For several days before that he had not taken any food or water. He knew that his end was near. I had gone to visit him, not wanting to lose these last few precious moments with him, but he looked at me, smiled and gestured with his hands, "Go to work! Go and do your work!"

We performed his final rites at the cremation ground in Khar. In keeping with his basic tenet of rootlessness, Swami Ram Baba had instructed us that there would be no particular spot of Samadhi, and that he should be cremated like an ordinary person. He had even told us that his ashes should mingle not in the Ganga but in the ocean. We followed his wishes. It was the biggest loss to me, but even today, if I have a question or a doubt, I address it to Babaji. The answer always comes.

The core principle of Swami Ram Baba's philosophy was to lose oneself in action, and this was something I had known, at a very fundamental level within myself, ever since my earliest days of struggle.

P. P. with Swami Ram Baba

Swami Ram Baba preached:

If you are poor - work!

If you are rich - continue working!

If you are burdened, with seemingly unfair responsibilities - work!

If you are happy - well, just continue to work!

Idleness gives room for doubt and fear.

If disappointment comes, please just work!

If your health is threatened - work!

When your faith and hope falters - work!

When your dreams are shattered and your hope seems dead - work!

Work, as if your life was in peril.

The truth is, your life really is in peril. So work!

No matter what ails you - work!

Continue to work - faithfully, dedicatedly and devotedly.

Work with Love, Faith and Patience.

Work is the greatest remedy

For every mental and physical affliction!

These words from my guru, teaching that it is through work that one can get closest to the divine, resonated with my own experience and belief.

6

GLOBAL FINOLEX

"When I think back, a strange feeling comes over me. We did not know the location. We did not know the product. When we began importing PVC, we only knew it was some kind of powder. We knew nothing about technology, had no money in our pockets. And there we were, talking and thinking of hundreds of thousands of crores! Certain thoughts and feelings had come to me. Opportunities arose through people I met. Decisions were taken. I felt that the land itself was calling me. More than ever, I feel that I was only the medium. None of this was MY creation."

For many years, Ratnagiri was just a name to me, a town south of Pune famous for its rare and delicious mangoes. My wife had established a family tradition, which in her absence is lovingly carried on by our daughter-in-law Ritu, to distribute boxes of mangoes on my birthday every year. For a great many years, this was my only connection with Ratnagiri.

Situated on the west coast of India in the south-western part of Maharashtra, the Ratnagiri district forms a part of the greater tract known as Konkan. It was such a piece of land in the town of Pawas near Ratnagiri, almost entirely barren, that was selected by Brigadier V.R. Khandekar and Mr. J.N. Pandit, who had been given the assignment to locate land for Finolex's PVC resin plant. The year was 1990, and Finolex had been a Public Limited Company for seven years already. I had spent the previous five years struggling, among other things, to get the government approval for a licence to manufacture PVC resin.

During the years of my little daughter's illness and suffering, the company had continued to grow steadily. Although my heart was elsewhere, my mind and body continued to function. The same inner strength continued to calmly respond to the guidance of an unseen external force. As before, opportunities continued to come my way. My thoughts and actions were focussed on growth, and growth did come to us.

The establishment of our plant in Ratnagiri brought us out of the middle segment and launched us as a fast-growing large-scale industry with foresight, power, and massive ambition. It was the turning point for the group. Things would never be the same again. We had now entered a new league, and had to gear ourselves up for a number of changes that were bound to follow.

There had been ups and downs in the past twenty years, but by and large our direction had been consistent.

By the mid-1970s our business and our brand were already well established. We continued to diversify into new products and technologies, and intensify our core business.

In the 1980s, the growth of our core products continued to boom. We now began simultaneously looking beyond these and allied areas, for new opportunities. We entered into joint ventures with foreign collaborators. Some of these succeeded, some did not. This was also the time when we took Finolex public, with great success.

By the time we entered the 1990s, we were ready for a quantum growth leap. My son Prakash, and K.P.'s sons Vijay and Deepak, had been working with Finolex for some years and were ready to lead divisions on their own. Time and again I instructed my people that product quality was much more important than sales figures. I knew very well that if we produced only good quality products, customers would flock to us, just as my grandmother and I had single-mindedly made for that crowded

Ratnagiri, 2006: Finolex Industries

Ratnagiri, 2008: India's first open-sea cryogenic jetty,
built in 1993

sweet shop in Shikarpur, knowing that we would have to wait our turn. So strong was the value that we had created that dealers in South India have personally told me that they would wait two months for Finolex products rather than offer an inferior brand to their customers! Adhering to the standards that we had set for ourselves had brought its own reward.

It was 1976 when we incorporated a new company, Finolex Plastics Pvt. Ltd., for the manufacture of PVC pipes. We set up our manufacturing unit at Pimpri on surplus land adjoining the cable factory.

We had had the equipment to make pipes right since 1958, with our first extrusion machine which was capable of giving an output of plastic tubes and rods of various sizes with the input of raw PVC. However, we had been busy, and totally involved in the production and sales of cables.

By the 1970s, the business was well established on a steady path of growth and we decided that it was now time for us to diversify into the manufacture of pipes. We had been hearing market reports that there was a rising demand for PVC pipes from the agricultural sector. This was a new product that apparently had the capacity to revolutionize the lives of farmers in our country.

The earliest pipes were probably made of bamboo, used by the Chinese to carry water as far back as 5000 B.C. Two thousand years later the Egyptians used the first metal pipe made of copper. Until the eighteenth century, when cast iron became relatively cheap, most pipes were made of bored stone or wood, clay, lead, and occasionally, copper or bronze.

When we began manufacturing PVC pipes, the majority of pipes used in India in buildings, in cities, and in the farms, were made of galvanized iron. However, PVC pipes had enormous advantages over the GI pipes. In many countries, the old GI pipes had been almost completely replaced by the new PVC ones, which were easier to handle, and provided transport for water and other liquid without seepage or wastage.

Switching from GI pipes to PVC was indeed transforming the lives of farmers. GI pipes were heavy and needed transport and weight-carrying mechanisms. The PVC pipes were so light that the farmer could load them on his bullock cart or even carry them himself.

GI pipes needed a plumber's expertise to lay and weld. PVC pipes, however, were designed in such a way that the farmer could not only lay them and the accessories himself but also gave him the freedom to change the layout as and when he wished. The new pipes were impervious to rust, and flexible rather than brittle as the GI pipes tended to be. The pipes that we sent out in the mid and late 1970s have stood the test of time and are still in service even today.

The only disadvantage was that there was an import duty of 130 percent on PVC resin and in this protected market, galvanized iron was much cheaper. Farmers had no choice but to allow water to collect in troughs where large amounts would be lost to evaporation. It took several decades before the government faced the reality that PVC pipes were not a luxury but a simple necessity that would bring water to the farmer. The duty was then reduced to a more realistic 5 percent, and finally farmers could pipe water easily into their fields.

Though PVC pipes have revolutionized agriculture, our cities are yet to make the shift. They continue to use ancient pipes made of cement to carry sewage and fresh water. In most countries, pipes in urban areas have been upgraded to PVC. Even within buildings, PVC pipes are now preferred in modern construction sites, to carry both hot and cold water.

In the early 1970s, there were other companies manufacturing PVC pipes in India, and they were all doing very well. Judging by the market for PVC pipes in the developed world, it was anticipated that in an agricultural country like India, the demand could run as high as a million tonnes per year. K. P. travelled to Germany to study pipe manufacturing technology at the Willy Anger machine manufacturing company.

The predictions that had seemed so fantastic to us in 1976 did eventually come to true. Finolex began to manufacture pipes and pipe fittings for every possible application – for agriculture, to carry hot and cold water in homes, to carry water and sewage in cities, heavy pressure pipes, and even pipes to duct telecommunication cables. Today India does indeed consume one million tonnes of PVC pipe per year, with an annual growth of ten to twelve percent. Finolex, the country's largest manufacturer of this product, turns out around 250,000 tonnes per year.

At that time, these figures were only on the boundaries of our hopeful imaginations. We imported one machine from Willy Anger, and then another. By now Finolex had reached the number two position in pipe manufacture, second only to Wavell India, a company which no longer exists. We retained an edge over them by using only the most modern and highest quality machinery and production standards. Our exports had earned us an import licence through which we could bring in the best and latest machinery. This ensured that our quality, speed, and the quantity of pipes we produced were much higher than those of our competitors.

As before, marketing continued to be my job while K.P. was in charge of production. We could see the huge rising demand for the product. We were addressing only a very small section of the market, and I knew that we would need to start producing on a much larger scale. We had spread comfortably over our land at Pimpri and for expansion would have to look elsewhere.

This next step came, as in the past, through a series of simple serendipitous events. It so happened that one day at a social occasion I met Mr. Vasantrao Patwardhan, the Chairman of the Bank of Maharashtra. We talked about my new business and ideas, and he casually informed me that a company which had started a shoe factory on eighty-three acres of land at Chinchwad, adjacent to Pimpri, had been unable to pay its loan and wanted to sell. It had a shed of around 50,000 square feet.

The very day after meeting Mr. Patwardhan at the bank, I made arrangements to visit the site and found it extremely attractive. It already had water and electric supply, good road connections and a godown. Everything was readymade. All we had to do was buy machinery and install it! We could begin production practically overnight.

We settled at a price of Rs. 2 crore for the entire land, building, and infrastructure, but to make use of this attractive offer I had to make an immediate decision. I had not had time to discuss the matter with any of the others, not even K.P., who was M.D. of Finolex Plastics, and was out of the country at that time.

Without a moment's doubt or guilt, I called my finance director and told him to come immediately with a cheque of twenty lakh rupees as advance to the bank towards a seven-year loan. The Chairman had the required documents prepared and with the board's sanction, made arrangements to hand over the property to us in the shortest possible time. Once again Mr. Mysore and Mr. Bhide worked on the legalities and other formal requirements to incorporate the new company. We later changed the name from Finolex Plastics to Finolex Pipes, and finally to Finolex Industries. Five acres of the 83 acres we bought was acquired by the Pimpri-Chinchwad Municipal Corporation (PCMC) in 1998 and recently another eight acres for road widening. Growth in Pune has been such that we have recently had an offer of Rs. 700 crore for the remaining seventy-eight-acre tract.

With this land, we were immediately able to start importing and installing machinery. Instead of restricting ourselves to just two lines we kept expanding until, by 1981, we had 13 lines of PVC pipe manufacture, along with pipe fittings of all types, including adapters, bulkhead fittings, caps, compression fittings, rigid couplings, flexible couplings, cross or 4-way fittings, 90-degree elbows, 45-degree elbows, and others. The company continued to expand, and the market responded favourably. By 2003, our production capacity had risen to 45,000 tonnes of pipe per year.

I often look back and marvel at the way things moved in sudden steps like this, with unexpected opportunities and quick decisions resulting in smooth growth and various events in our favour. Can one call it risk-taking? Or is it the result of intuition? For me, all my opportunities and all my decisions come from an unseen guiding force that even today continues to propel me forward.

By 1981, with the pipes doing extremely well, we brought them under the company Finolex Industries Ltd.

Some time in the year 1983, K.P. selected a product called jelly-filled telephone (JFT) cables which until that time had only been available

175

through import. He sourced technology from Essex in the U.S., and we began production.

In those days, there was a waiting period of twenty years and more to get a telephone line. Privileged individuals could hope to get a connection in ten years. Every year the monsoon damaged the old cables which were buried under the road, leading to a long period of ruptured phone services. The government had imported JFT cables and tested them between Bombay and Poona, and in some locations in the north. It was found that these cables were impervious to water and that they further improved the quality of communications.

The government-owned Hindustan Cables set up a new factory to start producing this miracle cable which would bring easy telephone communication to our country!

However, supplies from this factory were erratic and frequently delayed. We ourselves had been allowed a licence for only a small quantity. It took several months of follow-up, quoting tenders to the Department of Telecommunications, producing samples and so on, until we were given the required permissions.

With technology from the U.S., we began manufacturing the JFT cables. Our processes had been developed gradually over the years and they scaled up efficiently to support our increased volumes. This helped us to compete well with Hindustan Cables. Profitability was high, and a number of other competitors entered the arena. We were selling at the government price but our US collaborators helped us to maintain extremely high quality. Once again, expansion became an urgent requirement.

At this time, quite by chance, I happened to meet a Sindhi gentleman at a marriage party in Bombay who mentioned to me that he had a hundred-and-twenty-acre plot in Urse, Talegaon, along with a shed, and was thinking of disposing of it.

Today, a quarter-century later, the smooth and modern Mumbai-Pune expressway slices through Urse, and the Finolex plants are easily visible from a toll gate on the road. The old highway was rude and bumpy, and noxious with dust and diesel fumes. Urse was in the remote interior and could be accessed only through a rocky dirt road off this highway. Our jeep lurched and leaped, and the wind blew dust and grit at us as we rode towards it. With shaking legs, aching backs, and grimy faces, we stepped out but our hearts soared when we saw that this hundred-and-twenty acres of land was all in one piece. After discussing the matter with K.P. and our M.D. Mr. Talauliker we purchased the land outright at a price of Rs. 2 crore.

Developing this barren interior land was a long and difficult process. It had a large water body with a nearby source, and all the industries in the area could draw from it. But there was no electricity, and after much effort and time we were able to acquire a connection from the power station at Talegaon. Through our efforts, the nearby Urse village also received electricity.

By 1982 our new factory for a large capacity of JFT cables was operational on this land,and today there is a vibrant, modern community developing around it.

Business was expanding on all fronts. Growth seemed limitless. It was now time to take Finolex Cables public.

The Controller of Capital Issues (CCI) had the power to decide the premium share value of any company and ours was set at Rs. 18 for a ten-rupee share. I was appointed M.D. and Chairman of the company and my salary was fixed at Rs. 1290 per month.

I felt this was unfair because more than fifty percent of the employees in the company at that time were earning a higher salary. In those days, a company MD's salary was subject to a ceiling fixed by the government, but there was no restriction on the salary of other officials. Our Executive Director's package was around Rs. 8000 per month. However, the government had decided on this low figure for me based on my lack of qualifications.

I tried to explain that despite this lack, I was the one who had built the company up to this point from scratch. In vain did I try to put forward the many learned and experienced people from whom over the years I had learnt documentation, Finance, Advertising, PR, Marketing, Quality, and many other facets and skills of business that I had not been born with. The government was adamant. In their eyes, this was what I deserved.

This was not the first time I regretted my lack of education. Fortunately, I had some small personal savings, property, and investments from which I could expect reasonable dividends, and the low salary did not disturb my lifestyle to any great extent.

Our public issue was preceded by a series of press conferences and public meetings. Bombay as the financial capital was the focus of activity. We held a small event in Poona, at the Finolex headquarters, as well. After Bombay we moved on to other cities which had their own stock exchanges; Ahmedabad, then Delhi, Calcutta, and finally Madras.

Speaking in public to a large group for the first time, I was very nervous. I introduced our companies to the brokers, and described our background and origins. What gave me courage was the fact that we were already quite well known. Our products and our company had been highly visible in the Bombay press with large front-page advertisements since 1963. This history of twenty years gave us tremendous advantage. My dear friend Vaji Nariman Maloo had certainly advised us well! The press and market reports were excellent.

But it wasn't only our brand that was impressive. Our balance sheet stood up to scrutiny. Our profitability was high, turnover high and we had low equity. People could see that our products were long-term and our growth strategy had been sound and successful. Comparisons with competitors were also in our favour. The result was an overwhelming response and our issue was oversubscribed 64 times.

This huge reassurance and public support gave me great satisfaction. Now as a public limited company and with me as the officially appointed Chairman and Managing Director, we were no longer answerable to any individual but only to the company.

Bombay, 1983: P. P., Dr. Mukesh, Aruna
and Swami Ram Baba

I was now able to get good senior people on board, from the fields of banking, law and insurance, and their mature advice and guidance was very useful to me and to the company. We had Mr. G.V. Kapadia from New India Assurance, and Mr. Hemraj Asher from Crawford Bailey. The Bombay-based B.K. Khare & Co. took over as our chartered accountants and finance advisors. I had no experience of how to run a public limited company. Their support, and that of my family, gave me the strength and will to keep working in a positive way.

1983 was a very significant year for me at a personal level as well. This was also the year my daughter Aruna got married. Her husband Dr. Mukesh Katara is also from a Bombay-based Shikarpuri family.

All through Aruna's teens and as she entered young adulthood, our family had been preoccupied with Sonali's illness. Aruna had been a good student and had completed her education without any encouragement or input from me. Though she had graduated in the commerce stream, her preference was for humanities and she completed her Masters in Fine Arts. There had been a few occasions when I had taken her and Prakash on holiday abroad with me and that had strengthened the love we shared. After we lost Sonali, I realised that Aruna had been somewhat neglected and the emotional strain of continuously caring for a deeply loved sister with a fatal illness had given her great strength, but also made her more quiet and mature than others of her age and social status.

I began worrying about her marriage. Babaji reassured me that everything would turn out perfectly, and that I must visualise the most positive results. He said this to me many times, in many different contexts, and his reminder was always soothing.

We were unable to find a suitable match for Aruna in Poona at that time, and she was not keen on settling in Bombay. The quality of life in Poona is far superior to Bombay, and children who have been brought up with space, leisure, and greenery, would not prefer the Bombay lifestyle. We decided to travel around the country and first choose a city to Aruna's liking before we started looking for a boy. For a few months, I took my wife and daughter with me on business trips to various cities. In Bangalore, we spent time with Mohini's younger sister Kanta. All of us have always been very fond of her and her husband Shivkumar Wadhwa.

London, 1993: On a rare holiday with Ritu and Prakash

In every city I visited, they were looked after by the families of my business associates or by friends and relatives while I was working. Aruna then realised that Bombay, with its sophistication and cosmopolitan approach might not be such a bad choice after all! When we met Dr. Mukesh, there was no further hesitation from any of us and the wedding took place. Mukesh is the son of Dolumal and Hardevi Katara. Like us, they were also Shikarpuris who had fled Karachi at partition.

Mukesh, qualified as a dentist, owns the country's No. 1 dental lab business with laboratories in Mumbai, Pune, Bangalore, Hyderabad, Kolkatta and Delhi.

They say that each person brings his or her own destiny, and when a new member is added to a family, he or she brings a change in fortunes of the family too. I had seen that with each new member added to my family, there had always been a change towards growth, happiness, and luxury. First it was my wife and then each of our children. We bought our first car and first piece of land when Aruna was born. When Prakash was born, my business began to grow very fast with new projects and a new factory. When K. P. had got married, and when each of his children was born, the rise had continued steadily. Now with my son-in-law also I saw that great prosperity had come to us. At a personal level it filled my heart with happiness to see him take care of my daughter and watch her grow into a mature, capable and contented person. At the same time, in the very same year that he became a member of our family, the company reached a pinnacle of success by going public and being heavily oversubscribed.

Six years later, in 1989, my son Prakash married Ritu, also in a traditional arranged marriage. Ritu is the daughter of Gopichand and Sunita Hinduja. Gopichand's brother Srichand is married to Mohini's sister Madhu.

Mohini and I had known Ritu's family, and had been fond of her ever since she was a child. Both of us were simply delighted when the match was finalised. Ritu had been brought up in London and we realised that it would not be easy for her to make the transition into a joint family in Poona. We wanted her to settle down and find her own space, and tried our best not to oppress her in any way.

1989, Economic Times & Harvard Business School
Association of India Award for Best Corporate Performance :
Prakash, Mohini, P. P., Madhu Dandavate, K. P. Sunita, Deepak

For some years I had wanted to modernise our home, which was still just the way it had been when we bought it from the Shirodkars. But Mohini would always suggest that we wait for Prakash to get married, and then his wife could do it up just the way she wanted. As it turned out, Ritu has an inborn skill for design and over a period of a few years, transformed our old bungalow into a leafy, airy and beautiful home with a variety of spaces – some formal, some casual, some simple, some gleamingly modern, and some ornately traditional. She became a close part of our small family very soon, and brought a special warmth and caring for us which Mohini and I valued very much. On days when I was travelling to Bombay, she would wake early to pack breakfast for me to carry. Even today when I travel abroad, Ritu examines my itinerary in advance and packs for each occasion, labelling my clothes day-wise so that I don't have to spend time thinking about what to wear.

As with the others in my family, Ritu also brought her own karma of growth, happiness, and luxury. Soon after Prakash and Ritu were married, Finolex successfully made the quantum step into the big league of Indian manufacturing industries.

It is one of my greatest joys that the children in the family are well settled and contented. K.P.'s daughters-in-law, Priya and Vini, are extremely warm and affectionate. K.P.'s son Vijay married Priya in 1987 and they have two children, Rishi and Karan. His younger son Deepak married Vini in the same month as Prakash and Ritu. They now have two children, Radhika and Janak. We spend a lot of time together and being with the children gives me great pleasure. Our daughters-in-law are excellent cooks and very often prepare and send across special dishes for me. K.P.'s youngest child, Kavita, now lives happily in Bangalore with her husband Sanjay Raheja and their two children Sonia and Siddharth. I enjoy spending time with them on their annual visits to Pune.

Right through the 1980s, Finolex continued to thrash and struggle against the government with the issue of licences and raw material. We had some amount against our export licence, but it was never enough compared to our production capacity and the huge demand we had for our product. For a businessman in my position, it was like being forced by the government to live in a small room without sufficient light or air.

Pune, 1985: At Raj Bhavan with Rajiv Gandhi

It was in 1985 that I began thinking that it was time for Finolex Industries to start manufacturing our own PVC resin. At this time, we were importing large quantities of PVC resin against our export licence, and were still dependent on the government licence for our remaining requirement, which was very large. Besides the nuisance of struggling almost daily for the raw material, it would also save huge margins if we began producing it ourselves. I knew that it would be another massive struggle to procure a licence to manufacture, but well worth the effort once we got it.

As per the quota system, we used to get 20 tonnes of PVC resin per month from Nocil, 10 tonnes from Chemplast, and 10 tonnes from Sriram in Rajasthan (the DCM group). But we were consuming 400 tonnes of resin, acquiring the entire extra amount through import. It bothered me continuously that this was cutting into our margins. Our production was increasing, and not having a reliable source of PVC was hanging heavily on our profits.

To manufacture PVC resin meant involving ourselves in a different scale of activities and resources, of which we had no previous experience. However, I knew that it would be the right thing for us and that we needed to do it as soon as possible.

Around this time, I visited France as part of a FICCI[1] delegation, and met a gentleman associated with a French PVC resin manufacturer. When he heard that we were consuming 5,000 tonnes per year he became interested. I mentioned to him that we were thinking of manufacturing PVC resin ourselves. He was doubtful that an Indian company could do this. However, partly to help us, and partly because he knew that we would source at least some of our PVC requirements from his company, he issued a letter to me saying that he would be transferring the required technology to Finolex Industries which would give us the knowledge to manufacture PVC ourselves. I immediately approached the government with this letter, applying for permission to manufacture 30,000 tonnes of PVC resin per annum. The estimated cost of the project was Rs. 150 crore, an astronomical figure in the mid-1980s, and especially for a company with an asset value of just Rs. 3 crore.

---

[1] Federation of Indian Chambers of Commerce and Industry.

Once again I began the massive struggle to procure a licence to manufacture PVC ourselves, and once again began my trips to Delhi, applying, waiting, being rejected, applying again, trying every means within my power, completely determined to get the licence come what may. At this time one of the officials at Mantralaya who supported our effort was Anand Bhadkamkar.

It was not just my basic tenacious nature which saw me through this difficult period. Swami Ram Baba also assured me that I would be successful and that a chemical industry and a copper industry were surely a part of my future. This gave me the added strength to continue visiting Delhi five or six times every month, continuously following up during the rest of the time. It took nearly five years of performing this ludicrous, frustrating dance. During this time, the capacity had been increased to 60,000 tonnes of PVC manufacture. I agreed, even though this would mean doubling the originally estimated investment. Once again, before giving approval, the amount was raised and in 1990 I finally procured the licence to establish a factory to manufacture 100,000 tonnes per annum of PVC Resin. Without a second thought, I agreed.

When I received the letter of intent, my happiness knew no bounds. I took it at once and placed it reverentially in my pooja room! Along with a deep feeling of gratitude, I also felt somewhat overwhelmed at the challenging task that lay ahead. We would now have to begin raising money and developing a range of other resources. We would have to learn the technology, construct the plant, train people, and manage all the different aspects of this new industry.

By this time, the company was being managed by K.P. and me at the helm and our teamwork had improved even further. We were taking quicker consensual decisions and could go to the board for approval with much higher speed than before when other family members had been involved and time would be lost in discussion and passing papers back and forth.

We already had our own land, but this could not be used for the plant. I had never realised before that PVC manufacture had to be located on the coast! We realised afresh how little we knew of this new business

---

² Industrial Credit And Investment Corporation Of India.

we had embarked upon. While K.P. turned his attention to finding out about it, I now began my next big task – to source funding for this project which, because of the delay in issuing licences, was now valued at Rs. 350 crore. By this time, our factory making pipes was turning over around Rs. 12 crore, and the cable business only Rs. 18 crore. However, we knew that our industrial licence and our impeccable track record of growth were tremendously valuable assets.

I contacted ICICI[2] and prepared the application for a loan for the PVC resin plant. Once again this was a new, untried area for me and I needed to consult various investment bankers who were kind enough to help me with my proposal. I was warned that a part of the deal would likely involve a large chunk of equity.

ICICI Bank is today one of India's top retail banks with perhaps the largest customer base in the country. Historically, ICICI Limited was formed as an Indian financial institution in 1955 at the initiative of the World Bank, the Government of India and representatives of Indian industry. The principal objective was to create a development financial institution for providing medium-term and long-term project financing for Indian businesses. In the 1990s, ICICI transformed its business and began offering project finance through various outlets including ICICI Bank, its wholly-owned subsidiary.

ICICI was happy to see that we had our own land in Ratnagiri. It was an indication that we were sincere and committed to the project. The letter promising technology from France also showed that we had technology support and gave us credibility.

Our loan was processed through a syndication committee comprising three banks: ICICI, IDBI and UTI[3]. Since the application had been processed by ICICI, the dealing continued to be through them. To our great delight, an amount of Rs. 350 crore was sanctioned internally. However, we were told that Rs. 250 crore would be sanctioned in foreign exchange.

I was not experienced enough to understand what the implications of this decision could be. Before the official sanction letter was released

[3]   Unit Trust of India

188

by ICICI, I discussed these terms with my board. The rupee had been growing weaker over the last few years and I was confused. However, I was not someone who understood the complexities of finance and it was only a vague uneasiness that was bothering me. Dr. Neelkanth Kalyani who was now on our board offered to introduce me to his friend, Suresh Nadkarni, Chairman of IDBI who, he assured me, would give the best possible guidance.

Dr. Kalyani, founder of the highly successful Bharat Forge, was, like me, a Poona industrialist who had started from scratch, and moved from agriculture to manufacturing in the 1960s to set up a forging company that was now already one of India's largest. We got along well and valued each other, being part of a small and close-knit community who suffered the same oppression and anguish from the government policies and bureaucratic procedures, and stood by each other at every possible opportunity. At this moment, his help was greatly appreciated – and, as it happened, saved us from ruin.

There was no time to be lost because the matter was to be taken up by the ICICI board within the next few days. Without a further thought, Dr. Kalyani arranged a meeting for the very next day and took me in his private plane to Bombay, where we visited the IDBI building in Colaba together.

It turned out that Mr. Nadkarni was already aware of my application. He informed us that the board was to meet next day to finalize our proposal. He asked why we were accepting the foreign exchange loan, knowing that the rupee was depreciating. He asked whether I realised what the consequences could be. I explained that I was not very knowledgeable, and asked him instead for his advice.

Mr. Nadkarni now offered to replace the loan with a rupee loan from his own quota. He advised that I gave him a verbal request for this and follow it up with a written document the next day, he would explain at the meeting that the loan was now being given by IDBI, and in rupees. I agreed at once.

At the board meeting the next day, Mr. Nadkarni explained that the chairman and directors of Finolex had approached them for a rupee loan and IDBI was ready to give Rs. 200 crore. Of course this was a loss of face for ICICI which had gone through the pain of processing the application and approving the loan. We had gone behind them and approached another bank. They were annoyed but were graceful enough to cooperate with us in all the remaining formalities. This was business and India was slowly becoming a truly free country at last.

Within the next few days the Indian government announced a rupee depreciation of 54 percent and, just three days later, an additional 5 percent devaluation.

Since our loan was now in rupees, this depreciation had shot the cost of our project up.

If we had accepted the foreign exchange loan, it would have financed our project adequately. However, the depreciation in rupee value would have lost us equity and the seven-year repayment would have left us bankrupt.

Once again I felt that I had been favoured by providence. If we had been just one day late, we might have lost everything. I did not know much, but I had been uneasy that something was amiss, and once again I had been given good advice by good friends. The unseen force had helped me once again.

Our land in Ratnagiri was at Pawas. We had set up a team to locate the right spot and they had hired a boat and travelled from Alibag to Ratnagiri, in search of the perfect site. My instructions were to locate an area close to sea as deep as possible. I knew that this would bring us many benefits in the future. They took nearly ten months to survey the area extensively and when they submitted a report to me, we selected a place at Ranpar, on the Pawas bay. We later discovered that this had been a secret port of the British in World War II. Ranpar was an area designated by the government as "backward" and entitled our project pioneer status and several concessions, including sales and tax benefit up to ten years.

Besides its natural beauty and serenity, Pawas achieved prominence when an enlightened being called Swami Swaroopanand, a spiritual leader of great local influence, had made it his home. The place where he used to reside is now a peaceful ashram.

I now had to visit and see for myself whether this was indeed the right location for our plant. Pawas is a distance of about seven or eight hours by road from Poona and we found accommodation in a shabby little traveller's lodge in Ratnagiri around 15 km from Pawas. We had come by jeep because the roads were bumpy, and the land was rocky, uneven and pitted. It was around 6 o'clock on a chilly November evening, just a few days before Diwali.

A very old lady was sitting and cutting a thin branch for fuel. She sat on the path, blocking our jeep. My two colleagues and I approached her and spoke in Marathi. At first she did not reply. We requested her to kindly allow us to pass since it was getting dark and we had to go far. After a long moment's silence, she got up and stood aside. I saw that her clothes were shabby and she looked needy. I took a fifty rupee note from my pocket to give her but she refused to accept it.

When I insisted, she finally spoke. "Why should I take this when I have done no work?" she argued. I explained that I wanted her to buy Diwali sweets for her children. At this, she smiled and took the money.

Here was something I had always known – even if people were ignorant or poor, they always had guiding principles which made them behave in a certain way and differentiate right from wrong.

We continued to walk for around two hours through the scrub, exploring the area. By now it was almost completely dark and we lost our way a few times before finally locating the jeep, and we drove back to the lodge.

While walking through the land, I was filled with a strong feeling that this was the right place for our plant, that we must buy this land. I was convinced that a good factory would come up here and flourish.

We now began the process of purchasing land. It was important for us to have a large tract before we started construction. A chemical plant is not something that you can ever shift once you have built it! Over a period of six to nine months we acquired around seven-hundred-and-fifty acres in small pieces from a number of buyers. The land was barren, and the local farmers were pleased to get a price from us.

Now began the task of raising our industry from an asset value of Rs. 12 crore to Rs. 350 crore.

We knew from experience that the loan sanction together with the industrial licence made our industry an attractive proposition and put us in a good position to look for technology from any supplier.

K.P. began sourcing this, and spent days and weeks travelling. He ultimately selected Udhe GmbH, a German technology construction company to assist us with erection of the plant, and a process licence from their parent company Hoechst AG of Germany.

My brother worked very hard to set up this project for years together. He even fell ill because of his long 14 and 16-hour work days.

The Germans valued themselves at an hourly salary amounting to the annual salary of our people. They wanted a team of one hundred, but we made do with just eight or ten who gave us consultation, advice and technical drawings. The rest were Indians.

Between this team, they designed and built what we had intended; one of the world's best plants. The Germans were surprised to see what our Indian engineers were capable of. In the end, they were delighted to see that we had built something better than what they had in Germany in terms of size, amenities and products. Ours was one of the first such plants to come up and today German companies have great respect for our capabilities. India has hence become one of their important markets for manufacturing equipment.

The entire credit for managing and implementing the project goes to my brother K. P.

We began manufacturing PVC resin in 1993. The import duty also started coming down from 130 percent to 70 percent and gradually lower to just 5 percent. We started production with 100,000 tonnes per annum, which was further increased to 130,000 tonnes per annum.

Pune, 2006: P. P. Chhabria with Pratap Pawar and
Prime Minister Manmohan Singh

Our first cable exports had been to Iran and the Middle East where the requirements were very large. At that time, our major focus had been on gaining the benefit of government licence to import the raw material we required. For several years in between, our exports had floundered. In 1989 we had opened a full-fledged export department and through this increased focus, were able to send our cables out to Australia, Africa, the Middle East and several countries in South East Asia, until our export figure has now nearly touched Rs. 50 crores.

Today Europe is beginning to rely on India for its cable requirements. Some of our specialised communication cables, including fibre optic cables, have a distinct price advantage in Europe and the orders come in bulk, often to the tune of twenty or thirty crores of rupees at a time. In 2010, we crossed hundred million dollars – and we have still not even entered the American market. It seems that our exports may even exceed the huge and growing numbers we supply within the country. Regarding PVC resin, however, there is tremendous demand in India, and we are currently not considering exports.

Our capacity now stands at 300,000 tonnes of PVC per annum. The demand for PVC in India continues to rise. Today we are very satisfied to be number two in the manufacture of PVC resin in India. We believe that Finolex PVC surpasses all thermoplastics in versatility of processing and application possibilities. It is a validation of this belief that Finolex Industries has received the Top Exporter Award several times from Plexconcil, an independent body representing the exporting community of the Indian Plastics Industry, and supported by the Indian Government.

As the turn of the century approached, the world was changing fast. Technology had brought unbelievable changes in lifestyle. There had been unthinkable changes in world political geography. Climate had begun showing an alien and unfriendly side. The Indian government had initiated a process of economic reform that brought joy to the hearts of our country's businessmen! Bombay and Poona too had changed in many ways, not least of which was their names, now Mumbai and Pune.

It had been a period of change for me in personal terms also. It was an exhilarating feeling to finally be part of big business. In the entire period preceding this, K.P. and I had been in full control of every operational matter. We had done everything ourselves. This was no longer possible. Beginning the process of delegation and giving power to others now came to me naturally. I knew that this was very important. If I tried to retain personal control of each decision, growth would be impossible. I had good senior people who we trusted completely, and K.P. and I knew that the company was just as important to them as to us. We began the process of moving aside and gradually putting the company in their hands, now moving into more strategic, visionary, and guiding roles. My work hours and travel continued as before. At this time, though, the visits to Delhi reduced marginally, replaced by visits to financial institutions, banks and the state government.

At a personal level, I was now sought after socially and there was a feeling of satisfaction that even the most important and influential people in the country considered me a peer. However, though the number of party invitations increased significantly, my wife and I continued with our normal evening routine of walking, spending time with the family, and sleeping early.

These days when I see the youngsters who sleep late and wake late I realise that they are unaware of what they are doing to themselves. Even the ones who are serious and hardworking think it is fine to stay out all night partying on weekends. They do not realise the kind of damage they are doing to themselves. The human body is not designed for that kind of life but for regular meals and decent sleeping hours. It is hard to explain this to youngsters, and even more difficult to try and enforce it. They must awaken to it themselves or else they will learn, the hard way, that this so-called enjoyment is actually the worst kind of denigration of body and mind.

As our plant at Ratnagiri came up, we faced some resistance from the local people who were uncomfortable at the thought of a huge chemical plant in their neighbourhood. With the history in our country of the Bhopal gas tragedy, where carelessness led to loss of life, health damage, and terrible suffering, people are naturally wary and fear the consequences of chemical leakage and pollution. However, our plant has been designed and constructed in such a way that not a single drop or particle of any chemical leaves it, not even to go into the sea. I stayed at the site for days together and was finally able to gain the confidence of the people. Today our plant produces PVC of ten or twelve different grades, and is used not just for Finolex cables, pipes and plastic sheets but also by many other industries to produce all kinds of moulded articles including bottles, footwear, and films.

Since the raw material was now easily available to us, Finolex Cables included PVC sheets – rigid,corrugated and foam – in its product range. These provide any number of applications and brought yet another revolution in the construction business. We ourselves use this extremely versatile material for roofing and partitions in our own factories as we continue to expand.

Initially it was difficult to get qualified personnel for our plant in Ratnagiri. Our first engineers came from other parts of Maharashtra because the local people had neither experience nor relevant education, though we did hire all our clerical and administrative staff locally. This area was undeveloped and previously devoted only to agriculture and fishing. As more people came to stay, the local businesses also flourished and the place itself has become more developed.

We later bought forty additional acres in Ratnagiri town and built a housing colony for around 400 families. To make living here attractive, we landscaped the area with trees and lawns, a nursery school, library, and a clubhouse with a range of sports and other recreational facilities. While our plant was coming up, we constructed a guesthouse for our German collaborators to stay on site comfortably, in European style. We also acquired an area adjacent where, having taken care to select the greatest possible depth of sea, we were able to construct our own open-sea cryogenic jetty to enable economical and efficient bulk transportation of cargo at sub-zero temperatures. The jetty, the first of its kind in India, was given the American Concrete Institute's Award of Excellence.

Today Finolex is committed to developing Ratnagiri into a beautiful, modern city, one of the best in Maharashtra. Being close to the Konkan sea coast, it has many natural advantages. It is a pleasure for us to bring progress to the area and an improved lifestyle to the people.

Since 1994, we have arranged an annual weekend workshop for Ratnagiri doctors and send a team of prominent doctors with different specializations from Pune to conduct training sessions.

In the early 1990s, as our plant came up, K.P. and I travelled frequently to Ratnagiri, a tough eight-hour journey by road. We often had our German collaborators travelling with us. The long journey meant that even for a visit of a few hours, we needed to spend three days. This was when we decided that it was time for Finolex to have its own private plane. We selected a Beech Aircraft King Air, a popular model, and received permission for a private hangar at Pune airport.

A private plane seemed like affluence, but we had bought it out of sheer practical necessity. It got us to Ratnagiri in forty minutes. K.P. could fly there, work all day and the next day, and be back by evening. It also became easy for us to receive our international guests at Mumbai airport, and fly them to Ratnagiri within an hour.

On a few occasions, I used the plane to travel to Goa with Mohini. The irony of the situation filled me with wonder. I had been a boy who cleaned floors for other people. For years on end I had ridden about a bicycle scratching together a living. And here I was with a private plane at my disposal! How had this happened?

It had been a long, long time since I had thought about my childhood. Memories of the old days had been completely overshadowed by the events of my busy life. But it was at this time that I was lucky enough to get a chance that millions of other Sindhis and Punjabis like myself, displaced by partition, were never to get in their lives.

I was away, travelling in the U. S. when I was informed that I had been selected to join a FICCI[2] delegation to Karachi for a SAARC[3] committee meeting. Delighted to have a chance to visit my birthplace, I flew there at once via Zurich, landing at Karachi airport with mixed feelings. I felt both happy and sad to be visiting the home of my ancestors. I was also somewhat nervous at the idea of being in Pakistani territory!

---

[2] Federation of Indian Chambers of Commerce and Industry
[3] South Asian Association for Regional Cooperation

Many of us in the delegation had pre-partition links with Sindh or Punjab and the others also experienced the same feelings of nostalgia mixed with anxiety. We were given VIP treatment from the moment we landed. The Pakistani ministers invited us to their homes for meals, laying the tables with thirty and even forty different dishes!

I remember how surprised the Pakistani delegates of this area were when I spoke to them in my native Sindhi. They wanted to hear our stories, and we shared them in an environment of warmth and brotherhood, sitting and chatting late into the night. They did their best to make us feel at home, and plied us non-stop with delicacies of all kinds.

We were taken to visit Larkana, Lahore, and Islamabad, where we met Nawaz Sharif, who was Prime Minister at the time. I also visited Mohenjodaro, one of the earliest known human civilizations, which is a short drive from Larkana, the town whose courthouse I had had to visit as a child to recover my ten rupees from the Pathan who had stolen it. We were very close to my beloved Shikarpur, and I felt sad that the time we had was too short for a visa to be arranged. Our haveli and the streets of the city would have changed beyond recognition, but they live on as they were, in my heart.

When Finolex first set up in Ratnagiri, it was a very isolated area, without even a train passing through. Our country has been extremely well connected by the railways right since the nineteenth century, but because of the uneven and rocky terrain in this area, it took decades of planning before the Konkan Railway, which connects the two important port cities of Mangalore and Mumbai, came up in the late 1990s and made Goa easily approachable by rail. The Konkan Railway provides a spectacularly beautiful journey to travellers and has been a life-changing boon to people who live in this area.

While our factory was coming up, K.P. and I realised that many of our workers who were in the prime of youth had young children, who would soon require higher education. At that time, there were facilities only up to the 12th standard in Ratnagiri, and college education only in Commerce and Humanities. There was no engineering college in the district. We knew that we would need large numbers of engineers for our plant alone.

Mohenjodaro, 1994

I now applied to the government for a licence to set up a college of engineering and management at Ratnagiri through the Hope Foundation.

After a great deal of running around in Delhi and Mumbai for the permissions, which over the past fifty years we had become quite used to, we were given the go-ahead to start an engineering college under the Bombay University, through the All India Institute of Technical Education. By government decree, permission for mechanical engineering was given. Classes commenced in 1996. Today the Finolex Academy of Management and Technology is highly sought after for its facilities, its infrastructure and its highly qualified staff.

The first engineering college to be set up in the rural area of Ratnagiri in 1994, it is affiliated to the University of Mumbai and has sanction from Govt. of Maharashtra as well as All India Council for Technical Education (AICTE), New Delhi. The college offers four-year B.E. programme in the areas of Electronics, Electrical, Mechanical and Information Technology and has also introduced a postgraduate Master of Computer Applications.

Built on a 35-acre campus and funded by our Hope Foundation, it is one of the most modern colleges in the country with the best design, laboratory facilities, library, software, classrooms, equipment, and faculty. Our architects for the project were Banaji & Co. and even the interiors were lavishly designed. There are lawns and playgrounds. Students come from all over Maharashtra, largely Mumbai, and live in the hostel. Because of the lack of distractions in the surrounding area, it is an ideal place to concentrate. The sons and daughters of Finolex employees are given priority for admission. Various scholarships are offered to needy students.

Today Finolex is no. 1 PVC pipe manufacturer in India, and no. 2 in PVC resin. When I think back, a strange feeling comes over me. More than ever, I feel that I was only the medium. None of this was MY creation. It had come about spontaneously, through the gentle direction of my inner voice. Once success comes, it brings an intrinsic momentum, and wealth is generated on its own.

Ratnagiri, 1994: K. P. Chhabria with Sharad Pawar

Ratnagiri, 2008: Finolex Academy of Management
and Technology

Now that the manufacture of PVC resin had begun to settle and thrive, I began to look at other areas for Finolex to enter.

At that time, as today, there was a great power shortage all over the country. It looked like the situation would continue. Setting up a power plant would provide a much-needed service to the nation as well as a source of revenue for the company. At a power project conference in Kerala, I met a representative of the company Black and Veatch International of Kansas City, USA, a multinational organization specialising in consultancy to set up power projects.

We decided that we would set up a 500 MW power project. A site for the project was located in Kasargod in Kerala, a town adjoining the Karnataka border. We began the process of listing out all the terms and conditions. These things take time, and no decisions were forthcoming, but as usual I continued my follow-up.

The United States Secretary of Commerce Mr. Ron Brown was visiting India. Our economy was just beginning to open up and I realised that this high-profile visit would be a good opportunity to announce our intention and get a commitment from the Kerala government. The MOU was signed in the presence of Mr. Brown. Many industrialists and corporate dignitaries were present including Keshav Mahindra, Deepak Parikh, Ratan Tata, and others.

I spent many years following up, but things became very slow and no decisions were taken.

During that time, Dabhol was having its own problems. This huge Dabhol Power Plant had been set up in Ratnagiri to produce 2000 MW of power. It had been built jointly by Enron, GE and Bechtel. GE provided the generating turbines, Bechtel constructed the physical plant, and Enron had the responsibility of managing the project. In phase one, the plant was to burn naphtha, generate a capacity of 750 MW, and take it through to 2100 MW.

Meanwhile, LNG infrastructure and an associated terminal for LNG was also being erected, and in phase two LNG would be consumed to produce increasingly more power until capacity was reached.

Mumbai, 1994: Mohini, JRD Tata, P. P. & Prakash Chhabria

Dabhol itself was growing slowly and with all kinds of obstructions and pressure.

In the mid-1990s, however, a series of political events in India led to endless disputes over prices and terms of the deal, work slowed down at Dabhol and finally construction was stopped. Enron tried continuously to revive the project until 2001 when the company itself went bankrupt.

I had also begun the process of setting up an LNG pipeline to support our own power project as well as for other uses. We had even been issued a letter of intent by the central government to erect facilities for 2.5 million tonnes of LNG near the Mangalore port. I approached a large number of big oil companies around the world, but the Dabhol issue was fresh in their minds, and they were preoccupied with all that can go wrong in large-scale development projects when cultures collide.

Since our power project, which would have consumed a large amount of the 2.5 million tonnes of LNG, was also not making progress, we had to abandon this project as well. All the time I had spent, the energy of planning and sending out applications, and a lot of money were wasted in this process. Fortunately, our other companies were doing well in business, and I continued looking for fresh ventures to undertake.

This was the time when software was emerging as a big strength in India's skill repertoire. A small software company came to my notice. It was being run by a married couple at the Bhosari Industrial Estate. The company was looking for financial support and we decided to acquire it, and brought some well-qualified senior people to run it.

At that time, my idea was not just to run an offshore operation but to set up a centre for real software development. It was the right time to enter the software industry. However, the team given responsibility for this venture was unable to give sufficient time and energy for it to take off. The company's losses were later carried forward and transferred to a new company called I2IT Pvt. Ltd. I regret not having given my personal effort to this company, at least as much as I had to the power project, because I feel this would have made the difference and Finolex would have been a software power as well today.

I entered into yet another venture in the early 1990s that did not succeed, collaborating with the Dakota Aviation College in Canada to set up the Finolex Aviation Co. to provide training in various aviation-related areas including training for pilots, small maintenance of planes, flight-attendant training, and so on. We were given space in an airport in Kolhapur by the Government of Maharashtra. This project too did not attract the required level of focus from my team, and subsequently failed.

Yet another project I took up which had mixed success, was with AT&T to produce fibre optic cables. Soon after the process of liberalisation began, many multinational companies began looking to invest in India. With our solid base in the JFT cable business, we attracted their attention and we set up a joint venture to manufacture fibre optic cables. We were looking at a 50-50 partnership but they insisted on 51 percent, with only 49 percent for us. I was keen on the AT&T name which in those days was quite powerful. The factory was set up next to our factory at Urse and I was appointed Chairman of the Indian company. I travelled often to the U.S., attending board meetings at the AT&T headquarters in Atlanta every three months to formalise our expansion and future plans. However, the American counterpart made heavy losses and they sold their company in India to us. We bought hundred percent and merged it with Finolex Cables.

Soon mobile phones entered the arena and the government was considering privatisation. I approached AT&T, at that time the world leader, but they were hesitant because of the level of investment required. I travelled to the U. S. and met other telephone companies as well. Though there was some interest, the finance, which would have been at the level of hundreds of crores, became the main constraint.

Prakash and Deepak were also keen to pursue this opportunity. However, all of us were preoccupied with setting up and expanding our operations at Ratnagiri. It was a huge task, with huge problems and it was taking all our time and energy. It was nothing but a lack of consistent push that led to this effort petering out.

Urse, 2008: Vijay Chhabria

I regret all these failed projects very much. They represent the loss of tremendous business opportunities. In the areas of software and aviation training in particular, looking at today's booming market, I feel sorry that Finolex lost out. To me, the lesson from these failed projects is that when you don't put sufficient energy and time into a job, you will never achieve success.

In some cases, it was circumstances that contributed to the lack of success, and we had to write off our losses and move forward. In the case of the power project, it was not a complete write-off since we are today in the process of setting up a new and larger project on similar lines. All the learning we acquired in our earlier attempt will now be useful. In those cases where extra effort could have made the difference and resulted in success, the loss of opportunity continues to rankle although I never felt any personal sense of frustration or discouragement, either at that time or in retrospect. I knew that my role in the process was just to continue working and building. I always did, and continue to do so.

One of the satisfying successes we had during this time was our Israeli joint venture for drip irrigation. Finolex Plastro started with a Rs.3 crore turnover and has grown steadily, with an excellent future potential also. Besides helping farmers deal with the perennial water shortage, Finolex Plastro Plasson supplemented our PVC pipe business. Finolex Plastro Plasson is today one of the leading companies in the field of Micro irrigation in India having a turnover of Rs. 236 crores. We have a state of art manufacturing facility with a distinction of being the only makers of PCND drippers in India.

FPIPL offers a wide range of products and solutions in the field of precise Irrigation and Intensive agriculture cultivation. Our solutions include complete customised Drip and Micro Sprinklers systems and Turn-Key projects for All Agriculture sectors such as Row Crops, Horticulture, Green Houses, Plantations, Orchards, Nurseries and more.

During this time, Finolex also began to establish a presence in Goa. Ever since my holiday there with Joglekar and the two travellers from Mumbai in 1952, it had been one of my favourite places. In the years between, I had spent many holidays there with my family. Sales tax is not applicable here, making it an attractive place to do business. For years I had been tempted by the government concessions which invite industry to the state. Talauliker was from Goa, and I often told him to look for land for us when he went there on holiday. One day he came and told me that he had sourced a plot of twenty-five acres in Ponda.

This is how it came to be that in 1993 we collaborated with a company called Essex Wire and set up a plant, Finolex Essex Industries, to manufacture 60,000 tonnes of copper rods in Ponda, Goa. Essex had been part of a company called United Technologies, from which we had got technology for the JFT cables, and with whom we had had business relations for many years. Our production at Goa of telephone cables as well as of copper rods started, but Essex went into heavy losses in the U.S. and wanted to sell their interests in India to us.

I travelled to Goa often, and acquired twenty acres at Varna where we have built a factory manufacturing optical cables. We went into production a few years ago and with such a strong base in Goa, I built a beautiful home for the family near the beach on four acres of land.

In 1994, Finolex's GDR issue was a great success. This was an important milestone for the company. Talauliker and I travelled in Europe, the U.K., the U.S., Singapore, and the Far East for the road show. We visited many companies and once again our stock was heavily oversubscribed. We received sanction for a hundred million dollars, but were advised against issuing this amount as it would reduce our stock holding. We issued shares worth 55 million dollars GDR, which brought our stock down from sixty percent to a comfortable forty eight percent.

Today, Finolex is expanding heavily on its hundred-and-twenty acres of land at Urse, manufacturing a range of new products. Having reached a certain stability, I knew we could now extend the brand Finolex, nurtured and created to denote quality and reliability, to other products which could be quickly introduced all over the country using the same distribution channels.

High-tension power cables and switches were a logical extension of our current business and we have started manufacturing these using the same stringent quality standards we set for all our products. For example, industry standards require a switch to operate for at least 12,000 clicks. However, Finolex switches are tested for 30,000 clicks.

Besides these, we also came across a product that would support India's energy deficiency as well as the global warming crisis, and set up a line to manufacture energy-efficient compact fluorescent (CFL) lamps. They not only give the same light as a normal bulb but do so using only twenty percent of the power.

We launched this product with a capacity of about ten million pieces per year and today this figure stands at thirty million pieces.

Most important of all are my two new, enormous dream projects in the pipeline: a power plant and a port.

At Ratnagiri, we are in the process of setting up a 1000 MW power project which we expect to start within the next four years. The investment is planned at around Rs. 5000 crore. Bank loans have been sanctioned and financial planning done. When we first identified Pawas for our plant, my brother had purchased additional land with further expansion in mind, and the project will now make use of it. The process of putting together a team, and sourcing the best technology has begun. Once all this is in place, the project will be ready to roll-out.

Our port at Ratnagiri is a fair-weather port. We have started constructing a breakwater, and intend to develop it into a full-fledged all-season general merchandise port where ships can berth throughout the year. This will be the first private port in the state of Maharashtra.

The port, power and petrochemicals will work, supplementing each other, with scope for continuous growth & expansion, bringing progress, employment and creating wealth for the community. I look forward to witnessing successful completion of these two ambitious projects.

In April 2001, I experienced a great personal tragedy which left me alone and bereft. It was an unexpected blow and took all the philosophical strength I had to pull myself back to my routine and continue normal interactions with others as before.

Mohini and I spent our last holiday in Goa together in 2001. She had wanted to celebrate my birthday with just the two of us alone. It was one of our rare trips to Goa together and we enjoyed a peaceful, relaxing

Pune, 1996: Mohini and P. P. Chhabria

time. On the 12th of March she booked a table at a restaurant at the Taj Exotica and even arranged for a birthday song serenade for me at dinner.

We enjoyed the holiday so much that our daughter-in-law Ritu now decided that our whole family could get together to celebrate Mohini's birthday in Goa. This fell just a few weeks later, on the 16th of April. Ritu invited all the family members closest to us, and since there were too many of us to all stay in our home in Goa, we made bookings at the Taj. Flying to Goa from Pune was tedious since commercial flights went via Mumbai. We decided to make two or more sorties in our plane.

I arrived in Goa some days in advance and was walking on the beach one evening when I received a phone call from my son. Prakash was calling to tell me that his mother had taken ill and that I should come home to Poona immediately. It was the evening of the 9th of April.

It was already dark and though my children had taken special permission for me to land after the airport closed, I decided to wait till morning. However, I was uneasy all night, unable to sleep, wondering what was so serious that they had wanted me to rush home late in the evening. Even though I worried that something must be wrong, it was impossible for me to imagine what had actually happened. Next morning, the ominous feeling grew when I saw that my son-in-law Mukesh had come all the way to Goa to accompany me back to Pune.

Mohini had been admitted to the Ruby Hall Hospital, and I arrived there as soon as I could the next morning. I was allowed to visit her briefly. Immediately after that, the doctors pronounced that she was dead.

When I got home after all the rituals were over, I sat alone and tried to reconcile myself to this devastating event. I thought back with nostalgia on all the events of our lives together.

Mohini was just 63 years old when she died. In the past few years she had not been in the best of health, but we never imagined that there was anything seriously wrong. We had visited the Mayo Clinic in the U.S. for advice regarding her occasional bouts of back pain but they had examined her and said there was nothing wrong. I now feel that she may have needed good physiotherapy care, which she never received. I had bought her an exercise cycle from the U.S. which she used – but now I wonder whether that had done more damage than good. Perhaps all the years of care of Sonali, and her never-ending grief at having lost her, had left her with a weak heart. I do not know. It's true that Mohini was always looking after others, and as a result her own health must have been neglected. On the 9th of April 2001, she had suffered severe chest pain. If she had called for help immediately, and if she had allowed those at home to take her to a hospital, if she had been diagnosed and treated, perhaps her life could have been saved. I knew that it was useless to think like this. We humans make our plans, but we are always at the mercy of the greater forces, and nobody can predict what will happen even in the next minute. The best that we can do is to accept these events and take them in our stride.

As I had done when we lost Sonali, I went back to work almost immediately. Prakash, Ritu, Aruna and Mukesh were the greatest support to me.

It was only over the next few months that I came to realise how much Mohini had meant to me. She had managed everything and made my life simple, allowing me to focus on my work. She had shared all my burdens, and multiplied my blessings. I was now left alone, to cope with life as best as I could. She had been devoted to our home, and not interested in going out or socialising. She had never been much interested in material possessions. When we travelled, she would not want to go shopping but, being very fond of our garden, would look for plants she could grow and sometimes brought back packets of seeds or saplings.

Just a few weeks before her death, she had decided to give away all her jewellery, and distributed everything she had to others in the family. Over the years I had bought her a number of expensive watches, and beautiful saris from all over the world. I now watched with surprise as she gave away almost everything in her extensive wardrobe, and emptied her jewellery boxes, keeping only a bare minimum for herself. I now wondered whether she had had a premonition that she would be taken away from us so suddenly.

Though all of us knew Mohini to be an extremely kind and generous person, she had never bothered us with the details of what she was giving, and to whom. I now discovered that there were a large number among our friends, family, many of our staff and other less privileged people, who relied on her for financial help for medical or educational needs, and were now shocked and bereft at the sudden loss.

Mohini's brothers and sisters were all very close to my children. They all make the effort to keep in touch, sending lavish gifts and spending time with us whenever they can. We have always had very close bonds and I have always had a lot of support from all of them right through the years. Jyoti, and her husband Mohan Shroff, in Mumbai. She did all she could to reduce the pain of the loss, and over the years has made special efforts to talk to my children and visit, and send them gifts on festivals and days of celebration, when Mohini's absence is most deeply felt by all of us. Mohini's niece Usha has fulfilled the role of an elder sister to Aruna.

7

Hinjewadi, 2000

BUILDING THE FUTURE

"The irony that I, who have never had the benefit of formal education, can now be instrumental in providing education to hundreds of deserving and underprivileged students is unmistakable. It gives me great satisfaction that my contribution will leave behind something lasting for these youngsters and for the country."

It was some time in 1998 that the then Prime Minister of India, Atal Behari Vajpayee, constituted an IT task force, issuing a statement to the effect that IT was the future of India. The phrase "IT is IT", Information Technology is India's Tomorrow, caught the public fancy.

For the generation ahead, it is hard to describe the excitement of the approach of a new century. For us, it was not just the turn of the century, but a new millennium that lay ahead! As the long-awaited year 2000 approached, the world watched in eager anticipation, confident that change of all kind, perhaps even indescribable wonders, were in store!

It so happened that the year 2000 itself had spawned what became known as the Y2K Problem or the Millennium Bug. The Y2K fever had given India its first large opportunity to prove itself as a global provider of IT services. It was becoming a documented phenomenon that India was on its way to becoming a world leader in IT. We have traditional skills in Mathematics and conceptual thinking, and a large English-speaking population. The world was racing to embrace a host of new technologies. It was a heady combination! When the Prime Minister coined the expression "IT is IT", it filled us all with pride and expectancy.

It was at the annual general meeting of the MCCIA in the year 1998 that I first met Dr. Bhatkar. He had been invited to speak, and I listened to his lecture with great interest.

Padmashree Dr. Vijay P. Bhatkar is well known for his achievement and service to the nation in various IT-related areas. Dr. Bhatkar had just arrived from Delhi, where he had attended a meeting of the Prime Minister's IT task force which constituted eminent people from different fields.

In 1998, India had already achieved exports worth five billion US dollars. Considering the rate at which the Indian IT industry was growing, the panellists had felt that the aim should be to take it from five billion to fifty billion in ten years time. This was an ambitious and highly attractive proposition, one made even more attractive knowing that it would be unmatched by the growth of any other industry in any country in the world!

At that time, the office of the Prime Minister had launched this proactive Swadeshi movement with the specific intention of launching India as an IT superpower in the emerging global village. However, as Dr. Bhatkar told us, the upbeat mood of the task force was dampened when one of the participants, the Chairman of the HR panel of the working group, posed the question "How?" For IT to grow, quality manpower was an urgent necessity and for this it was essential that we scale up our education in technology.

After the IITs and RECs (Regional Engineering College) were set up, there were no comparable institutions providing education in the higher technologies. At that time, the number of students enrolling in colleges of computer science or computer engineering was also limited. One solution, it was felt, was to set up a new chain of IITs with a focus on IT, and these would be called "Triple-I T".

Listening to Dr. Bhatkar as he appealed to the MCCIA members to come forward and fund such an institute, I felt overcome with a strong sense of the guiding force bringing me yet another opportunity to achieve the goal of widespread education that I had long been striving towards.

After the meeting, I approached Dr. Bhatkar and told him that I would be interested. I told him about the Finolex Academy of Management and Technology at Ratnagiri and that I would be extremely interested in creating a similar institute to provide the highest quality education of that type in areas of advanced technology.

Dr. Bhatkar was delighted at my interest, and prepared a high level design for our meeting the next morning. He warned me, however, that in the fifty years of Indian Independence, no private initiative had funded an institute of the stature that we were discussing. Even the magnificent TIFR, TISS and IISc had been promoted by the Tatas who had donated the land and infrastructure for these institutes, but they were ultimately run entirely by the government. However this did not deter me since I knew that in other countries, particularly in the U.S., private foundations have indeed created the finest institutions.

At this time, there were a large number of private institutions in India providing training courses on programming languages and specific areas of technology. Graduate level or diploma level knowledge and training were also available at thousands of centres around the country.

When I was very young, school had seemed nothing but a tiresome chore to me. As I grew, I had realised how precious education was. Now, at this stage in my life, I had observed that hordes of young people from middle-class families were leaving to study in the U.S. Why should they have to spend so much and go so far away for a good-quality education?

I decided to go ahead with a full-scale campus providing high-technology education at the graduate and postgraduate levels. We decided to keep the "Triple-I T" concept which would infuse the teaching of advanced technologies with the academic standards of the IITs. However, since we wanted to give the institute a global positioning, our triple-I T would be the International Institute of Information Technology. We also felt that "triple-I" was too casual and decided that our institute would be named "I-square IT" which conveyed a more sober, scientific impression.

I knew that the investment would be immense and there would be no returns for a long period, but I felt confident that it would eventually become self-sustaining. We would start by establishing ourselves in Maharashtra, then make a name at the national level and sooner or later, we would be internationally recognized. I could think of no more worthwhile project to be funded by the Hope Foundation which was later renamed as International Institute of Information Technology.

IT was an area that fascinated me. We began looking for land for our institute at Hinjewadi near Pune, one of the major centres of software development in our country. Our idea was to build on twenty five acres, but the government sanctioned only ten. Adding three acres over the next two years, we have already occupied the entire FSI. Once again I found that the best pieces of land had been allotted to others. What we were eventually given was a totally rocky stretch, one that had been unwanted by anyone else.

My daughter Aruna was becoming increasingly involved in this project. She now began to spend a great deal of her time and effort to nurture I²IT and bring it to the global level we had envisioned. We roped in Hafeez Contractor, architectural creative genius, to design our space. Hafeez is a very positive person and he assured us that he would create spaces within the building rather than merely a building on the space we had. Using an unconventional style, he built a giant roof, a structural challenge which creates a tunnel effect of wind that has made the entire area self-cooling. The structure has been designed in such a way that with the thousand students on campus today, and even with another thousand over the next few years, the feeling of space and freedom will continue to dominate.

Dr. Bhatkar also began the process of designing a programme specifically on IT which maps the entire spectrum of IT and IT-empowered business management. Our programmes included Robotics, Nanotechnology, Stem Cell Biology, Molecular Medicine, Nanobiotechnology, Microelectronics & VLSI Design, Embedded Systems Design, Networking and Telecom, Wireless Technologies and Advanced Software Technologies that covered Multicore, Multiprocessors, Clusters, and Grids. We also launched programmes in the areas of Computational Fluid Dynamics, Automotive Engineering, and Oil and Gas Engineering.

I²IT, 2004: K. P. Chhabria, Dr. Vijay Bhatkar,
Azim Premji, P. P. Chhabria

It was a massive challenge to put together this body of knowledge, and to write a syllabus that would stand up to the scrutiny of international experts in the field.

Once again, setting up the institute was a source of great learning for me. Even though industry is growing at a tremendous pace, not many venture into academics. It became a challenge to attract students to our institute. We tried various means, involving people from industry and from other universities, and gradually our student rolls grew and still continue to grow. We were well aware that in other countries, graduate and postgraduate students come to academia only with the support of fellowships and research grants. It was important for me that bright students at every economic level in this country should avail the exceptional facilities at I²IT and we made provisions for scholarships and assistantships for meritorious yet underprivileged students.

Finding faculty was another uphill task. By the nature of the effervescent IT industry, the best personnel are highly sought after and attrition is high at every level. Finding professors with doctoral qualifications is always difficult, and even more so in IT. It took a long time before we settled with a team of highly competent and committed faculty.

This was not the end of our problems. By the year 2002, it had become clear that the "dotcom" bubble had burst. We had just begun our institute, offering a postgraduate diploma when the shockwaves of the downturn brought an end to the euphoria in the IT industry. Dozens of small IT companies and number of IT training institutes in the country, closed down. It was now even more difficult to find students.

However, I understood very clearly that the future of the world and our nation, was closely linked with IT. It was not possible for these advances to be reversed. The current crisis was a result of highly inflated expectations collapsing. Our expectations were simple and realistic: to provide high-quality education. We had always known that returns would take time and we were in this for the long term. We continued to press on, ignoring the sense of despair around us and confident that there would soon be a revival which would have far greater depth and relation to reality. We continued to invest, building a new hostel and continuing to seek collaborations with international universities.

Finally, I²IT came into being as an autonomous institute, and was dedicated to the service of the nation in May 2003 by the then President of India, Dr. A.P.J. Abdul Kalam, himself an internationally renowned scientist.

There was no indication at this point of what would happen next. On paper, the economics did look good but, as with the other ventures, it was purely experimental. As with my other ventures, it was only the continuous external guiding force that kept me moving ahead.

After offering high end technology programs for 11 years, I²IT launched undergraduate programs in Engineering under the University of Pune. Today the Institute offers B.E. in Computer, Information Technology and Electronics & Telecommunication. Presently, there are more than 500 students on campus and the 1st batch of young engineers will graduate in 2015.

Looking out at our beautiful campus today, I do feel confident that we are moving in the right direction. Our hand-picked faculty is as committed as we are to bringing the best to our students. Unlike many other private institutions whose courses are conducted by visiting faculty, the staff at I²IT are full-time and avail all privileges including Provident Fund and even insurance. I feel that this makes them more secure and committed and ultimately gives the students a better benefit. We have been fortunate to attract this team of highly competent professionals.

Our aim is to groom not just a new generation of professionals with IT skills but also the next generation entrepreneurs in a global setting. In the short period of a few years, we have even researched, developed, and patented two of our own products. We have been approved by the Pune University for doctoral research. To be the most modern high-technology institute is a continuous process which requires international alliances, and constant research associations.

Over the years, I²IT has admitted a substantial number of international students from Korea, Iran, Nigeria, Sudan, Thailand, France, China, and Indonesia. The fact that students from advanced countries come to India to learn from us is a matter of great pride and indicates that India is becoming recognized as an advanced country.

I²IT Hinjewadi, 2003: President of India Dr. APJ Abdul Kalam
with P. P. Chhabria

It was a matter of great honor for me when the prestigious Hunan Vocational College of Science & Technology, China appointed me as "Honorary President" in recognition of my contribution towards education in India. The granting ceremony was held at Hunan Vocational College, Changsha, China in early April, 2011.

Aruna is now fully involved with I²IT and as the President handles overall administrative and strategic affairs including finer operational details for which she has a knack. She oversees functions in Finance, Administration and HR. As time passes, I feel proud to see her management and leadership qualities flowering.

The Government of Maharashtra also allocated us an ITI college to manage. The ITI or Indian Technical Institutes are a praiseworthy initiative set up by the Indian government all over the country soon after Independence to provide vocational training to students. We agreed to take responsibility for the one in Ratnagiri and of have upgraded it with a view to providing the best quality education at this level. Students will have the additional benefit of access to the faculty of our engineering college there. We have also set up a new Central Board English medium school in Ratnagiri which is funded and run by my daughter-in-law Ritu in the name of the Mukul Madhav Trust, named after her little baby who passed away when he was less than three months old.

The irony that I, who have never had the benefit of formal education, can now be instrumental in providing education to hundreds of deserving and underprivileged students is unmistakable. It gives me great satisfaction that my contribution will leave behind something lasting for these youngsters and for the country. It is many years since I ran away from my studies to play marbles and fly kites with my friends, and I look back with great satisfaction at my contribution towards education.

As I²IT developed and grew, my work at Finolex Cables and Finolex Industries continued as before. Expansion continued.

We always felt that our workers were a part of our lives. K.P. worked side by side with them and knew them personally. I knew each employee by name when our team was of a few hundred. I cannot make the same claim today, because we now have more than five thousand employees, and I'm also no longer directly involved in the plant. At that time, I made sure I made at least one round every day. It's extremely important to be a part of the shopfloor, to understand people's needs and the interpersonal dynamics they share. We have always placed full trust in our people, knowing that it is they who run our company. They are there around the clock, and no one watches them when they work at night. We leave everything in their charge, knowing full well that they will do absolute justice to the trust we place in them. We understand that smart professionals take their jobs very seriously, because that is their life and their livelihood. There's no need for us to try to interfere. Good management consists in finding good people and letting them do their job as well as they can with proper guidance but not constant control.

We had a clear understanding that education and medical facilities were just as important to our workforce for themselves and their families as it was for us. One of our initiatives was to give monetary donations to their children's schools and colleges. We also gave large donations to some selected hospitals so that our people would get priority treatment. Our people were entitled to take holidays on those occasions specific to their religion or community without any kind of discrimination. Some time in the late 1980s, I developed a six-acre plot of land in Pimpri which I owned personally, and constructed housing colonies where I gave priority to Finolex employees to buy apartments almost at cost.

The best learning comes from the line. It's the workers, supervisors and managers who work on site. If you are free and open with them, they will tell you more and you will learn more. We understood that HR must certainly maintain perfect records, discipline and every level of confidentiality. But for us empathy was also extremely important, perhaps more so than for others because we ourselves have come up the hard way and seen every level of struggle and discomfort.

Years ago we implemented reward programmes for good suggestions. Everyone knows how important it is to have avenues through which your people can approach you with their feedback, problems and suggestions. What is equally important is to make yourself approachable by spending time with them, listening and interacting. We never restricted our communication only to HR or senior managers.

Right until 1998 I punched my time card along with the other workers at the factory. Everyone would know that I had arrived, and arrived on time. It happened occasionally that a senior person would join the company and find it beneath their dignity to punch a card, but if the Chairman is doing so, then the act loses its indignity. After all, we are all workers, working towards a common cause – to build a great organization.

During recruitment, we never looked at a person's community, or tried to find an affinity of language or relationship. We never favoured vendors who were known to me personally, but left their selection to the professionals whose job it was to do so. Similarly, we have never recruited relatives in our group, and even our sons who have joined have entered at the level of stores and workshop, and come up the grades with learning and output reviewed at each level. They too continue our traditions of closeness to the people we work with, always conscious of their needs and wants.

When my son Prakash was born, all the family members, particularly my mother and grandmother, were delighted that I had a son. As he grew I began to observe that he was very much like me in many ways. He had the same quick grasp of new concepts. In material terms too, he was not fussy and preferred simplicity in clothes and belongings.

He was a good student and after he completed his schooling, was keen to continue his education in a boarding school in the U.K. where his cousins, K. P.'s sons, had been studying. After completing the course there, all three boys went to the U.S. for their graduate degrees where they studied subjects of their choice.

When the boys came back, they all joined the company at the lowest level. Prakash worked first in Stores where he got a good understanding of all the materials. He did all the jobs at that level, including carrying wooden cases and packing them with cables. After a year, he did a stint in the Accounts department and then in Purchase. Deepak and Vijay apprenticed at Bajaj Tempo for six months, working on the shopfloor. They later joined Finolex and moved through each department, working their way up from the bottom.

After a few years Prakash moved to Finolex Industries to work under K.P. We had big plans for the company, and wanted his participation in the growth and direction. K.P.'s sons Deepak and Vijay now came to work with me.

Because these boys have worked their way up from the bottom, they understand every functional area and whenever required, can work alongside the team or provide training or inputs. They continue to eat their meals in the factory canteen along with all others.

In 1983 we began a morning ritual that continues till today. This was a daily half-hour meeting where all the senior plant managers would sit together with the senior administrators, finance personnel and heads of other departments, and discuss the second and third shift of the previous day. The relevant person would note what action was to be taken on each of these issues. If purchase was unable to secure bearings required by one department, another department might be able to provide them temporarily. While sharing problems, solutions came more easily. Decisions would be taken immediately. There was no memo or indent required or any process of getting signatures which would waste time. The output of these meetings resulted in immediate action. This practice continues very successfully till today.

We had initiated computer accounting in 1978, and our system of MIS was automated when we implemented SAP as early as 1989, second in Pune only to the Tatas. At that time, we were going through a phase when we were unable to retain good CAs in our finance department. We found that they all wanted to work with large companies, or run their own practices. Implementing SAP was an easy way to automate and make the systems independent of people. SAP takes time to assimilate into an organization, but in around two years and with an enthusiastic team, all systems had been streamlined.

In our search for people, for us long-term relationships are extremely important and we would rather let even the most brilliant candidate go if he or she has a track record of job-hopping. Shortage of manpower at every level of skill will continue in this country as our economy continues to flourish. People have options and they have a right to these options, they keep industry more dynamic.

Pimpri, 2008: Deepak Chhabria

While selecting lateral employees, I always ask why they are leaving their current job. Is it only because of money? Do they give some frivolous reason? If someone tells me that he wants to move from a larger company to my medium-sized organization where he will be closer to management, or if he wants to join because my factory is close by his home whereas his current workplace takes him an hour to get to, these are good, practical answers.

I normally make recruitment decisions very easily. The "yes" or "no" comes to me very clearly. This is probably a result of my many years of management and life experience. Of course I have made mistakes.

A large company will always have a wider pool of better qualified and more experienced people to choose from. But for us it was always a challenge we looked forward to, training people to work together with us and make a powerful and cohesive team. I believe that every employee has the potential to be the perfect member of my team, and it is my challenge to guide them accordingly.

K.P. worked at the plant all the time, along with his team, laughing and joking and eating his meals with the workers. I feel that this is one of the reason we have been so successful.

Because of our own experience, we never limited a person's growth by his education or his background, and looked only at his abilities and attitude. Many of our people grew from small beginnings right to the very top of our company. At Finolex, growth is directly related to performance. Of the many of my team members who I will always remember, one is Shalini Soans, who worked as my personal secretary for more than twenty-five years. She became unwell and was finally diagnosed with cancer and had to leave. The company looked after her right till her end.

After Shalini, my secretary was a young man from Hyderabad, Sridhar Reddy. He was a graduate engineer and while working with me also completed his MBA. He was an efficient and very sincere person and though I relied on him to make my functioning smoother, I was always conscious that this man was in the wrong job. With his qualifications,

Chinchwad, 2008: Prakash Chhabria

his aptitude and the quality of energy he put into his work, he deserved a much higher position. Over a period I had him transferred to the Marketing Department where he continued to grow and was promoted to Senior Manager, then General Manager, and today he is President Marketing, drawing five or six times the package he had at the time of joining. There are many other cases of employees who have been transferred or promoted when the right opportunity arose, and as they have grown, both they and the company have benefited.

Many of our employees have remained with Finolex for the entire period of their working lives. I remember Ballu Jaisingh who joined Finolex in 1960 before our first plant was started in Pimpri. He continued until retirement and we extended his tenure even after that. All his three sons joined Finolex, and I'm proud to say that they continue to be part of the Finolex team.

There are many other such examples and it is them to whom Finolex and I owe our success.

When people have been with the organization for a length of time, they understand the culture and the people. By promoting and retaining them at the market salary, both benefit. It is a matter of pride to me that many employees at every level and in every department have stayed with Finolex from entry right until retirement. One of our peons, Padam Singh, worked with us for forty years! Our company driver Naik retired after more than thirty-five years of service. Mukhya Joshi was one of our earliest employees. He could not hear well and was not able to talk but his work was perfect. He handled the Stores and was a cheerful and dedicated person, working continuously and never wasting time. Even after his retirement he comes to wish me at home on my birthday every year.

It is not possible for me to name each one of my people individually, but I value each one greatly. A large number of them have been silent workers, putting in their efforts without any great display or showing off what they have done. They continue to do so with dedication and commitment, and it is they who have brought the company to where it is. As Finolex now completes fifty years of existence, I feel a special gratitude towards them. Many continue a close association with us,

Mumbai, 2006:
Aruna Katara receiving the
Maharashtra State IT Award
on behalf of I²IT

inviting us for their children's weddings and taking care to inform us of special events in their lives. We have recently begun the practice of continuing with our people after retirement, offering them consulting or training assignments.

I would like to urge youngsters to understand the importance of this long and warm association which may not give short-term results in terms of money or operational results but can be immeasurable in helping you to build your future.

It's hard to imagine that we had started in the 1960s with a quota of one and a half tonnes of PVC and one tonne of copper. Today we produce 260,000 tonnes of PVC resin per annum. Our copper plant produces 30,000 tonnes of copper rods per year.

Our very first industrial equipment, the copper braiding machine we had installed at the cowshed at Kakakuwa Mansion occupies pride of place in a special glass case at the reception area of our plant at Pimpri. As a policy, we always bought our plant machinery from the number-one reputed supplier with the logic that if the plant is good, productivity will be good, too. K.P. and I both believed, and continue to believe, in the most modern equipment. Even our workers feel happy that we have the most modern and best designs.

So many industries work hard and struggle, as we did. So many wind up and close down due to lack of support, marketing, finance or other reasons. It's very hard to understand what caused us to flourish as we have done. I have never felt that this great creation is something I did myself. It has just happened naturally. I met the right people, made the right decisions, worked in a creative way with a positive outlook, always looking for new opportunities. I was lucky to attract people who formed a dynamic team and worked with me towards common goals. There is nothing extraordinary that I have done that others have not done.

In recognition of my accomplishments; of rising from my simple beginnings to building one of India's leading business enterprise, I received an "Award of Honour" from The Prime Minister of Israel Mr. Ehud Olmert at a grand ceremony in Jerusalem during the Prime Minister's Conference for Export and International Cooperation, in 2008. But I truly believe that all this success is due to special blessings

Pune, 2008: Dr. Mukesh, Amit, P. P.,
Aruna, Mowgli, Amrita

which I am not able to understand or explain, which I accept with greatest gratitude and humility.

I am happy to pass it on to others. Besides the systems and discipline that K.P. and I have laid at Finolex, we have also built up a strong and dedicated team who run and manage the company with skill and commitment.

We understand and respect the responsibility we have to our investors, employees and all the stakeholders of Finolex and have been careful to groom our successors to develop the competence they require to take over this responsibility. We have never made the mistake of allowing our emotions to influence our management decisions.

I have now relinquished my position as Chairman and reins of Finolex Cables is now in the able hands of Deepak who is now the Chairman. K.P., too has retired and Prakash has become the Chairman of Finolex Industries. I am content in the thought that in my absence, the companies will continue to flourish on their own. Though I am not involved in any operational details, I do continue to attend office and execute my daily activities.

I leave behind my foundation of discipline, uncompromising product quality, a commitment to technological advancements, and the highest quality of manufacturing facilities. It was at the core of my business philosophy to always invest in the best technology, offer quality products to the customer, control rejection and rework, provide an excellent working environment to my staff and managers, and to work with strong systems, and the most advanced business and management tools.

Some years ago it ceased to be important for me to understand new technological advancements. I have full faith in the abilities of those who follow me. Qualified, experienced and dedicated professionals that they are, I know that they will take the right decisions at the right time. There is no one-person authority. The company will continue to run, long after K.P. and I are no more.

People have remarked that I am a quiet, inexpressive person. Inside, however, I am always thinking. I see no need to speak or display

Pune, 2008: Hansika-Hiya, Ritu, P. P., Prakash, Gayatri

emotion unless I have something relevant or important to say. As my age advances, I find myself becoming more detached. I don't dwell on any particular achievement or wish for any particular possessions. For years on end I travelled long distances on a rented bicycle. Today I have a private plane I can use when I want. The irony amuses me. I hold no particular store by either. I live in a comfortable home with people I love, who love and respect me. My greatest joy is to spend time with my grandchildren. Aruna's daughter Amrita graduated from Boston in 2011 and completed her MA in Media and Communication from London in 2013. She is tall and good looking; a fine, accomplished young woman and very creative.

Her son Amit completed his Bs.BA. from Suffolk University in Boston in 2009, and I was pleased when he came back to work at Standard Chartered Bank in Pune. I feel those two years gave him a good grounding in discipline and experience of a professional work environment. He is a sharp and intelligent young man and now, after three years of working at Katara Dental, enjoys his role looking after Marketing and travels almost fifteen days of the month. He reminds me of my younger days when I used to travel so much. Amit is engaged to Dr. Samita Moolani who is an eye surgeon.

I enjoy regular holidays with Amit and Amrita in India and abroad. I find it interesting to talk to them and learn about how they perceive the world, what their interests are and how young people think these days.

Prakash's daughters Prakita and Hansika went to school in Pune. On weekends we played together and I enjoyed listening to their stories about their friends and all that they did during the week. Prakita is now pursuing her BBA at Symbiosis. She is a talented musician and continues to practice. I love listening to her play.

Hansu is still in school and good at art and craft. We have interesting discussions which we both enjoy.

My home is spacious, peaceful, and surrounded by greenery. The food I eat is light and nutritious, the clothes I wear simple and neat. For nearly three decades I have walked every evening for an hour in a garden near my home, and a session of physiotherapy exercises has been added to my morning routine.

My association with the sky continues, and its vast impenetrable expanse continues to fuel me with the power to envision and strive to complete the two new projects.

All my life I have followed the practice of waking early, working all day, and sleeping early, which I continue to do. To wake early is to experience a freshness of the spirit. When you walk alone in the fresh morning air, nature walks with you and speaks to you, bringing you ideas, energy, and the courage to make quick decisions.

If the story of my life told in these pages is able to inspire readers to believe that it is possible to grow from a Rs. 10 service person to a Rs. 10,000 crore entrepreneur, it will bring me great satisfaction. I do not want anyone to feel poor, or crushed by conditions which appear too difficult, or too depressing to work or try something better. All the life experiences I have gathered can be summed up in some simple values for youngsters. 'Never get dejected when faced with hurdles. Always think positive because every challenge or hurdle one faces is an hidden opportunity." One must always strive to grow; but with quality in mind and sincerity in heart.

Being poor or lacking can never be the reason for not trying to pursue your dreams. Even if you are not the first ranking student in your class, you are still capable of creating and innovating. You are still valuable. If you live in poor conditions today, remember, that can surely change too. Only you have the power to change your karma.

London, May 2008 : Chairman of the UK-India Business Council Lord Karan Bilimoria presented the silver platter at a function organised to celebrate the launch of the 1st edition of this autobiography.